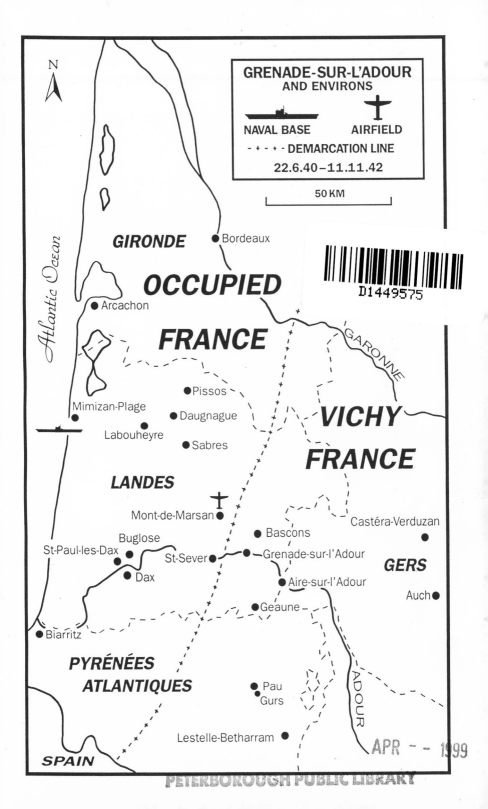

JUST RAOUL

The Private War Against the Nazis
of Raoul Laporterie, Who Saved Over
1,600 Lives in France

JAMES BACQUE

Prima Publishing
P.O. Box 1260BAC
Rocklin, CA 95677
(916) 786-0449

Prima Publishing
Rocklin, CA

Library of Congress Cataloging-in-Publication Data

Bacque, James, 1929-
    Just Raoul: the private war against the Nazis of Raoul Laporterie, who saved over 1600 lives in France / by James Bacque.
        p.   cm.
    Includes index.
    ISBN 1-55958-142-5
    1. World War, 1939-1945—Underground movements—France—Bascons Region. 2. Laporterie, Raoul. 3. Bascons Region (France)—History. 4. World War, 1939-1945—Refugees. 5. World War, 1939-1945—Jews—Rescue—France—Bascons Region. I. Title.
D802.F82B382   1992
940.53'44—dc20   91-31143
                                                             CIP

---

92 93 94 95 RRD 10 9 8 7 6 5 4 3 2 1

Printed in the United States of America

Permission is gratefully acknowledged to *The New Yorker* and writer Harvey Sachs for the right to reproduce a paragraph from the article "Der Ordinaire" about Hans Deichmann, which appeared on June 4, 1990.

Cover photograph of Raoul Laporterie: Laporterie Archives

Maps: Page Active Design and Elisabeth Bacque
Typesetting: Tony Gordon Ltd.

Published by arrangement with Stoddart Publishing Co. Limited, Toronto, Ontario.

To Madame Laure
and
Irène

Pour les parents,
les enfants du monde sont tous
des frères et des soeurs

———•———

"Love" is a verb
sometimes wrongly used
as a noun.
— John F. M. Hunter

OTHER BOOKS BY JAMES BACQUE

Fiction

The Lonely Ones
Creation (with Kroetsch and Gravel)
A Man of Talent
The Queen Comes to Minnicog

History

Other Losses

Plays

Judgement Day

Contents

Acknowledgments *vii*

Introduction *1*

Note on the text *3*

Chapter *1*   Gallia Est Omnis Divisa in Partes Tres   *5*

Chapter *2*   Saving the People   *18*

Chapter *3*   Growing Up Landais   *35*

Chapter *4*   Anarchist in Office   *50*

Chapter *5*   Spreading the Net   *57*

Chapter *6*   The Worst Winter of the War   *72*

Chapter *7*   A Dangerous Comedy   *83*

Chapter *8*   Vive de Gaulle   *93*

Chapter *9*   The Joy of Goodness   *104*

Chapter *10*   Bauführer Laporterie   *117*

Chapter *11*   The Burning of Grenade   *127*

Chapter *12*   A Night of Liberty, a Dawn of Sorrow   *136*

Chapter *13*   The French and American Death Camps   *147*

Chapter *14*   Where Is Peace?   *159*

Epilogue   The Modest Millions   *170*

Notes   *181*

Index   *189*

Acknowledgments

To THE PERSEVERANCE, courtesy, humor and courage of Raoul Laporterie, many hundreds of people and this book owe their lives.

Peter Hellman of New York generously advised and helped me at the beginning, as did Jack McClelland of Toronto.

The friends I made while living in Grenade-sur-l'Adour are many and warm: Dominique and Nicole Houdy, who helped in many ways, especially with the manuscript; Mme Laure Laporterie, Irène Duvignau, Jean Louis Terzi and many others. To Colin and Viviane Cusack of Spéracèdes and Jean-Claude and Susannah Ellena of Paris, many thanks for the boundless hospitality. To Albert Yaeche of Bordeaux and his sister, Huguette, of Biarritz, to Daniel Castel of Bordeaux, to Joseph Haim of Cannes, the sisters Esther Levy and Rivka Cassutto of Tel Aviv, to André Tachon of Toulon and Henri Vinet of Pau, all my thanks. Philip Hallie of Connecticut generously lent me a photograph of the André Trocmé family, and shared his knowledge of Le-Chambon-sur-Lignon, including the amazing story of the German officer named Schmahling who saved refugees. Charles Wittenberg of Toronto also gave me a wonderful story, that of the distribution of leaflets in Toulouse by his Resistance network in 1941–44. Odette Guitard of Spéracèdes generously shared her specialized knowledge of the period, as did Jean Pouzelgues of Paris.

I am grateful to the helpful staffs at the French Military Archives, Vincennes; the Public Records Office, London; the Bundesarchiv, Koblenz; the United States National Archives, Suitland, Maryland; and the archives of the towns of Thorée-les-Pins, Labouheyre, and Buglose. Special thanks to Raoul Laporterie for the use of his personal archives, and to Sarah Halperyn of the Centre de Documentation Juive Contemporaine, Paris.

The wonderful John Robarts Library in Toronto deserves special mention, because the staff are so uniformly helpful and knowledgeable about their superb collection.

I also owe thanks for generous help to Bill and Helen Robson of Toronto, to Madeleine Barot, Mme Sarah Halperyn and Gilbert Lesage of Paris, and to Peter C. Newman of Victoria, and to Erika Dessauer-Nieder of Seattle. To Nelson Doucet and my editors at Stoddart Publishing, and to Michael Marrus and Jessica Daniel of Toronto, many thanks for advice and help. As always, my wife, Elisabeth, was inspiration, support and guide when I needed all in abundance.

J.B.
Toronto
April 1990

Introduction

DURING THE WAR, my mother often sent me to the post office in Toronto with letters or parcels for people we knew in prison camps in Germany. That was a word I hated and feared.

So I felt kinship with Raoul Laporterie when I read an account of his saving about 1600 refugees from Nazi terror during the war. I loved that story, which appeared in one chapter of *Avenue of the Righteous*, by Peter Hellman of New York, because it revealed to me a man who resisted oppression without violence. This seemed to me a parable of the twentieth century: one man in a defeated country who refused to give up, won 1600 victories against the enemy.

Hellman's account was necessarily short because he wanted to include as many stories as possible of Christians who saved Jews from the Nazis. Sensing a full book in this, I went to France to interview Laporterie himself. My publisher at the time encouraged me, so in 1986 I settled into a small villa outside Grenade-sur-l'Adour in southwest France, bought a bicycle and went to work.

In all the stirring stories about Laporterie that I later collected were several recurring motifs. He enjoyed what he was doing, despite the danger, which added a salt of risk to the savor. He was also tenderly concerned for the fate of his refugees after he had brought them to safety. His friendships with some of them lasted far longer than the war.

In Laporterie's extensive archives, I came upon the strangest story of all, first hinted in a few letters and postcards to Laporterie from a man in Germany named Hans Goertz. Laporterie told us that he had taken Goertz and another German prisoner named Adam Heyl from a French army prison camp in Mont-de-Marsan in 1946 to work in his store there. The prisoners had been made available by the French government to men like Laporterie to repair damage done during the occupation of France. But these letters and postcards went on for years after Goertz's release, always expressing his affection for Laporterie. Side by side with them in Laporterie's files were similar letters, full of devotion, affection, and respect, from the Yaeche family and others — Jews whom he had saved.

Now I was forced to go to Germany, or else allow my prejudice to overcome the obvious need to do research there. In fascinated distaste, I crossed the Rhine to Bonn, where Hans Goertz told me the story of his capture and suffering, and his emergence into the hands of his savior, Raoul Laporterie.

Having studied the stories of many French people who saved the lives of others at the risk of their own, I have no doubt that what Laporterie did flowed naturally from common human sympathy, always apparent everywhere, but exposed by the war like a spring by a bomb. All over France, as Nazis and some French people chased Jewish refugees to death camps, hundreds of thousands of French people in sympathy gave food, shelter, money, transport, identity — in a word, love — to the persecuted. After the war, farmers, villagers, merchants, priests, pastors and ex-soldiers all over France helped their former enemies as they emerged half-dead from the French army camps. There was no hatred then.

Note on the Text

THE RESEARCH FOR this book was conducted mainly by interviews with survivors, but also through archives, chiefly the personal archives of Raoul Laporterie. I have been influenced by the admiration I felt for Laporterie on first reading about him. This has caused me to suppress, at his urgent request, certain personal details that he found embarrassing. I regret that the reader has been denied this aspect of the story, which is therefore somewhat less than truthful. Everything that does appear in the book is as accurate as I can make it.

The manuscript, originally in English, was translated into French and read over by Raoul Laporterie, André Tachon, Albert Yaeche and others of Laporterie's family and friends. Thus they approved and corrected the narrative together with the dialogue. I devised most of the dialogue from letters or discussion, and some was supplied orally by the original participants. All the dialogue has been read and approved by at least one participant in the conversation. The whole manuscript has also been read by Madeleine Barot, who experienced some of the events described. Odette Guitard, who lived through the war in France, read all and corrected some of the manuscript. Parts of the manuscript were read by Jean Pouzelgues, who also participated in some of the events described.

Because many people important to this story have died since

1945, because it was dangerous to create records in the period from 1940 to 1944 and because some personal papers have been lost, certain details, such as first names, are missing. In some cases, anecdotes are fragmentary because the police tore people away from each other, leaving no forwarding addresses. In some cases, stories remain fragmentary because the participants knew no more than fragments themselves. In the Resistance, knowledge was confined as tightly as possible, so that no single person could reveal by betrayal or torture more than the bare minimum needed for his or her work. Time, like the Gestapo, has wiped out lives, annulled memory, leaving us with blanks that only imagination can fill.

1

Gallia Est Omnis Divisa in Partes Tres[1]

FRANCE WAS divided in three parts. Adolf Hitler seized the rich north. Philippe Pétain took the poor southeast and the empire. Charles de Gaulle in exile kept her honor. A nation that had been fiercely independent for a thousand years fell in a few weeks to Hitler's blitzkrieg.

On a hot morning in the middle of June 1940, as the battle in the north of France went on, Raoul Laporterie stopped in the cool gloom of the front hallway of his home in Grenade-sur-l'Adour to kiss his wife, Laure, goodbye. "I'm going to Bordeaux to see Bezos," he said. Laure looked at him, alarm on her beautiful face. Bordeaux, 150 kilometers away, the refuge of the government that had fled Paris, had just been bombed. "I have to do something about these refugees. I'm obliged," he said, surprised that she should question him even by a glance.

Laure was amused because he said "I'm obliged" even when he was going to a bullfight. In the arena, on the street, Laporterie campaigned ceaselessly along the road of his ambition, public service. He had organized shelter for hundreds of Alsatians recently moved by the Paris government out of their homes in the danger zone of Alsace where the Germans were expected to invade, and now he had been placed in charge of a mission to take care of further refugees streaming south ahead of the invader. In his pocket rustled a letter headed Ordre de Mission, which read:

> Mr. Laporterie, mayor of Bascons [his home town, a few kilometers east of Grenade], is assigned to arrange with the civil commissioner of the railway station at Bordeaux [principal city in the *département*, or province, of Gironde] the transfer to the *département* of Landes [south of Gironde on the Atlantic coast] of evacuees. He is asked to gather information on the origin, number and date of arrival of evacuee groups. Civil and military authorities are asked to accord him every facility for the accomplishment of his task.

It was signed by the secretary general of the evacuee service.

Laporterie probably saw refugees passing as he backed his new beige Renault Juvaquatre into the brilliant sunlight to turn north through Grenade. For days now they had been coming from the north past his home, on the main street of the town. Laporterie had organized shelter in Bascons for Alsatian families at the outbreak of this war. As the mayor of Bascons and *conseiller d'arrondissement* (county councillor), he had persuaded his childhood neighbors, friends and relatives, who made up most of the 500 villagers, to take in more than 100 of the Alsatians. But there were probably ten million more refugees now on the road, many of them farther from home than they had ever been in their lives. There was no plan for them as there had been for the Alsatians. A hunted people heading anywhere away from the Germans, they were hungry, tired, frightened, in need of gasoline, food for themselves, feed for their horses, medicine, shelter, news, parts for their cars. The national state was collapsing all over them, so the local governments were rescuing them. Laporterie was like a man on shore who sets out in his canoe to rescue passengers from a sinking liner. The canoe in this case was the little Juvaquatre, four doors, forty horsepower, in which he was dodging refugee carts danger- ously fast under the green ceiling of plane-tree leaves on the road from Grenade to Mont-de-Marsan.

From Mont-de-Marsan he took the train to Bordeaux. The man he was going to see was an old friend, Dr. Robert Bezos, whom he had helped to elect as the deputy at Paris for his district in Landes. Laporterie was an excellent organizer, so lazy Bezos often asked him to go up to Paris to do his office work for him. Laporterie was flattered but not awed by his sudden importance in Paris. He was forty-three years old, a big success in Landes, but he still thought of himself as a *petit bonhomme du pays qui est sorti du village* — a little guy from the sticks.

Bordeaux was jammed with soldiers, refugees, government clerks, who crowded the streets, filled the hotels and restau- rants, sleeping on floors, in the parks, on top of loaded wagons. Laporterie found Bezos among the unhappy-looking deputies emerging from a futile meeting in Anatole France high school, and the pair squeezed into a restaurant for lunch. Laporterie lit a cigarette and ordered a Noilly on the rocks. Bezos described the situation, likening it to the worst part of the First World War. The parallels were ominous: Paris was threatened again, so the government fled to Bordeaux again; the army collapsed again, so, once again, the government appealed to the British, the Canadians, the Americans to save France; Marshal Philippe Pétain, who had saved France at the last minute in 1917, was now recalled in old age to perform the miracle again.

"But what happened?" said Laporterie, who had been a soldier himself alongside his father in the first war.

"They had more tanks, more planes, more trucks, more everything than we did," said Bezos.

"But I just saw dozens of fighters and bombers on the

runways at Mont-de-Marsan," said Laporterie. He knew there were also thousands of new GM trucks in a depot just north of Pau.

Bezos shrugged. "You see the roads," he said. "How could we get reinforcements to the front through so many civilians? Anyway," he finished with a fatalistic shrug, "it's all over now."

"No," said Laporterie angrily. "Everyone thought it was over in seventeen, but we stopped the Boche then." He was proud that he had fought beside his father in the trenches at Verdun to stop the greatest of the German offensives.

"It's over, Raoul," said Bezos. "We can't stop them on the Marne this time — they've already crossed it."

"What about the marshal? What does he want to do?"

"He will probably hand France over to Hitler."

"No."

"Otherwise, we go on fighting, more people die and then Hitler takes it anyway."

"But that's the end of France."

"Yes, that's the end."

All that he and his father and millions of the dead had saved in 1914 –18 he saw being swept away now in a few weeks. He felt especially helpless because he had just heard that his young brother had been reported "missing, presumed captured." Laporterie himself had suffered through illness and starvation in a German prison camp in 1918, and the thought of Jean-Marie enduring the same filled him with anguish.

"We can't just give up," he said. "We have to hold on."

"To what?"

"To France."

"France is beaten."

"*I'm* not beaten, by God," Laporterie roared.

"Are you going to start a revolution?"

"No, of course not. I'm loyal to the marshal. But I will not give in to the Boche."

The small man, impeccable in a correct gray suit with a correct handkerchief, was talking so loudly that people turned their heads.

"You know I don't usually get angry," said Laporterie hotly, "but when I'm in the right, I'm terrible. And I'm in the right." He moved his head furiously, thumbed his lapels proudly.

Bezos was taken aback. "All right, I know something you can do right away," he said. "My friend Oppenheimer from my office in Paris — you remember? Abel?"

"Yes," said Laporterie. "Tall, droll fellow. Very well dressed. Well educated."

"He's on his way down here. Will you help hide him?"

"What for?"

"He's a Jew."

Merignac airport to the southwest of Bordeaux was bombed that night but not destroyed. The next day, General Charles de Gaulle got into a plane lent to him by Winston Churchill to fly to England, and several dozen French warplanes took off for the long flight to North Africa, where some members of the French government still hoped to hold out against the Germans. The French in North Africa did not resist the Germans, but de Gaulle, with Churchill's help, formed a nucleus of refugees who soon organized the Resistance that began to harry the Germans in France. These were the two leaders in the West most determined to oppose Hitler. De Gaulle, a middle-ranking officer in the French army through the thirties, had repeatedly given warnings about the very military disaster France was now experiencing, just as Churchill, then leader of the opposition in Britain's parliament, had warned his own countrymen. Both men had been largely ignored.

The defeat of France had actually been brought about by the ruling classes in the government and the army, who were seeking personal advantage at the nation's expense. The government's policy was contradictory, appeasing Hitler because the leaders feared war, while preparing for war because they feared Hitler could not be appeased.

The French were not alone. The destruction of the League of Nations, the Russian alliance with Hitler, the sacrifice of Czechoslovakia showed that nobody in Europe would give up anything for peace — except the freedom of others. So, afraid of war but unwilling to give up war as a policy, wanting to win the war but afraid to continue it, the men of Bordeaux could only do what Europeans had done for centuries in such crises: postpone the fighting, not end it.

Pétain, whom Laporterie deeply admired, was alone as the supreme power in France at the moment when France had become powerless. This tough old soldier, who had rallied the army in 1917, had only a few sterile ideas about France, among them the conviction that the nation was now to be punished for its past sins. In his speech of Sunday, June 16, 1940, warning of the impending disaster, the fall of France, he began by praising the army whose deficiencies had brought catastrophic defeat on the nation. He said that this was because the enemy was "superior in arms and numbers," which was not true. He referred smugly to France's having "fulfilled our duty to our allies," which was not true, because the government had asked the British to relieve France of the obligation. Then he said, "It is with a broken heart that I tell you today it is necessary to stop fighting." Surely, even to an old warrior, the end of fighting is a relief, if not a joy. Yet he said he regretted the armistice, while he said nothing about the fall of his country to the invader. He asked everyone to be loyal to him, and to be led only by their faith in the fatherland, whatever that meant. About half the brief speech praised the incompetent army. There was nothing to encourage the French to stick to their faith that French civilization could survive despite Hitler. The story is told to this day in France that all across the country people raised their fists to their radios and roared, "We are betrayed!"

The cynicism of the rulers of Europe was probably never more evident than in the negotiations between Hitler and Pétain. It was clear now that under Pétain the government of France was more interested in government than in France. Hitler, who could have taken all of France, but not the fleet or the colonies, stopped to make a deal with Pétain. He would leave a poor forty percent of the country unoccupied if Pétain would neutralize its fleet and colonies. Pétain got the right to govern a corner of France, in a sort of house arrest, in exchange for removing from combat the only means he had to help liberate France. For the job of governing France from Vichy, Hitler conceded to Pétain an army of 100,000 men mounted on bicycles. The government of Vichy was thus from the first hour a German fist in a French glove.

The underlying reason that nations cannot disarm was exposed in the debris of France's collapse. By arms nations defend themselves; by arms nations are governed. Every army threatening a foreign enemy also threatens domestic opposition. Hitler allowed Vichy's army to exist for one reason: to protect Germany from the French. Weygand, commander in chief of the French army, defined it perfectly in June 1940 while his army was collapsing in front of him. To de Gaulle, who had been encouraging him to fight on with fleet and empire, Weygand said, "But that's childish. . . . Oh, if only I were sure the Germans would leave me the forces necessary for maintaining order."[2]

In the week of the fall of France, the rules of war and peace were changed forever by the signature of one man. President Franklin D. Roosevelt, seeing much further ahead than his fellow Americans, knew what the thunderheads over Hitler's Europe meant for the United States. As France fell and the

British staggered back bleeding from the continent, the walls protecting America were being smashed. Roosevelt decided that America had no more time. On June 27, the President took the unusual step of signing an executive order to implement part of a congressional bill in advance of the rest. He named Vannevar Bush to head the new National Defense Research Committee, ordering him to get to work immediately on "new devices of warfare," which the President had already decided must include the atomic bomb.

As the Germans took power in Paris, where Frédéric Joliot Curie had been doing some of the most advanced work in the world on splitting the atom, all of France's heavy water, a critical component in nuclear reactions, was being loaded on a ship in Brittany to be transported first to Britain, then to Canada, so that research could continue on building the atomic bomb.

Laporterie and Bezos left Bordeaux early the next day in Bezos's car. Laporterie looked around, glumly seeing Bordeaux free for the last time. The treeless streets echoed, the iron balconies looked down onto the cobblestones like empty opera boxes. They took the narrow roads southeast through the sandy plains of Landes, where the peasants still wore wooden clogs as in medieval times.

Toward noon, they stopped at a restaurant they knew well. The proprietor was listening to the radio proclaim the news of the armistice that Pétain had just signed with Hitler. As they were finishing their meal, motorcycles roared into the narrow street and stopped. The door opened and in walked four dusty German soldiers. One of them said, *"Bonjour, messieurs, mesdames"* rapidly to everyone in the room, as is the custom in the south of France. No one spoke. The proprietor nodded at them without moving from behind the bar.

The French-speaking German motioned for the proprietor to come over. He stood near the Germans' table.

"The restaurant is closed," said the proprietor.

"But everyone is eating. It's not late," said the German.
"It's because we just ran out of food," said the proprietor.
Laporterie and Bezos continued to eat.
"We'll just have what they're having," said the German. He
was speaking perfect French in the accent of the region. He
pointed to Laporterie and Bezos, who were having omelets.
The rooster was crowing in the courtyard. The Germans
obviously knew that no restaurant in rural France ever ran out
of food. There was no further resistance the owner could
reasonably offer that the German could not argue down in a
moment. He turned away to get the food. Laporterie and Bezos
got up to leave the silent restaurant. Outside they found their
car hemmed in by the German motorcycles.

Bezos was senior to Laporterie under the hierarchical French
social code because he was a doctor and a deputy, but it was
the nervy Laporterie who immediately took the initiative. He
walked back into the restaurant and up to the table where the
Germans were still waiting to be served. With his usual courtesy, Laporterie spoke the first words he had addressed to a
German since he had been their prisoner in 1918. The soldier
politely apologized for having detained Laporterie, got up
immediately and went out with one of the other soldiers to
move the motorcycles.

Laportierie and Bezos drove on.

"They speak perfectly," Bezos said.

"They're SS," said Laporterie. He had seen the death's-head
insignia on the collar of the uniform. The SS were shock troops
who led Wehrmacht attacks. Every one of them took an oath
to defend Hitler's life with his own. Every one wore his blood
group tattooed inside his left arm so that doctors could give
him blood immediately on the battlefield. Five thousand of
them had been sent to seize Mont-de-Marsan because of its air
base, where there were still French army planes.

"You can bet they're not seeing the place for the first time,"
Laporterie said, recalling the tourists in leather shorts they had

seen these past few years, ostensibly come to climb the Pyrénées.

Few French people believed that Britain could withstand Germany, which was the strongest country on earth. Few people had heard of Charles de Gaulle when he broadcast his message of resistance to the nation from London on June 18, 1940. To the majority of Frenchmen, it seemed that there was no hope anywhere in the world. Britain was finished, Italy had stabbed them in the back, Russia was Hitler's ally, America didn't care about France, Japan was allied with Germany and Italy. So they followed Pétain in the dim hope that they could save a few of their ideals by compromising all of them. In despair, the members of the Chambre des Députés of France had simply abdicated, leaving Pétain to cope with the ungovernable Hitler. Pétain's minister, the famous toady Premier Pierre Laval, was soon trying persuade Hitler to accept France as a partner in the Thousand Year Reich, but Hitler took what he wanted from France, ignoring Pétain and the armistice.

The bewildered were soon the indifferent. Philosopher Jean-Paul Sartre spoke for many French people when he wrote that he wanted to live "without hope." The historian Marc Bloch wrote, "We find ourselves today in this appalling state, that the fate of France no longer depends on the French." This was because for too long the fate of France had depended on the French.

The armed resistance abandoned by the government in despair was replaced by the clandestine Resistance of a few unarmed individuals determined to save whatever they could from the wreckage.

A few days later in Mont-de-Marsan Raoul Laporterie parked his car in the narrow street fronting La Petite Maison, the chief of the four clothing stores he owned in the area. Around the corner in the Place de la Poste, the main square, the city hall bore the red (white) and black flag of Germany, as did the post

YELLOW

office across the street. German soldiers had moved in to run all the civic affairs of Mont-de-Marsan, including the telephone, post office, local government and police forces. All the French officials were cooperating with them, according to the terms of the armistice signed by Marshal Pétain. Established at Vichy, Pétain's government retained only a weak amount of control over Occupied France. He could do nothing to prevent the Germans from annexing the provinces of Alsace and Lorraine, which had been taken over by the French in 1918. The painful irony of paying the Germans to occupy the country was enforced by the armistice. As Laporterie walked into the post office to collect his mail, he saw the first of the posters that the Germans were putting up to discipline the unruly French. One said: "Frenchmen, clean your houses. Sweep your courtyards." Another showed an Aryan Wehrmacht soldier smiling handsomely at a doubtful-looking dark-haired French child he was holding in his conqueror's arms. The legend instructed the "abandoned" French to trust the Germans.

In the post office Laporterie greeted his friend Mlle Renée Darriet, who ran the telephone switchboard.

"You have mail like a cabinet minister," said the clerk behind the counter, handing him a bundle of letters far bigger than he had ever received before.

In the dim little office above the main La Petite Maison, Laporterie read the mail, which was multiplied by the disastrous events in France; all the extra letters were requests for help. A Mme Breton, living at Bucy-le-Long, in Aisne, wrote:

Sir:

I am the widow Breton, mother of Corporal Charles Breton, who sent me your address so you could pass some letters across the line. Therefore I am sending this little package of letter paper, and if you wish I will also send a money order for him, as well, but I await your reply first, because think how hard it must be for a mother to know

that her son is without money. I am counting on you, and
if you could ask him if he needs some linen I will send him
a package. I'm counting on you.

Mme Veuve Breton

Others letters said, "I am sorry to bother you, but in the hope
that . . . I wish to join my wife and two children . . . My friend
and I are in a camp in Gers, but we could get demobilized . . .
We suffer from missing our family, whom we wish to rejoin . . .
with the deepest thanks . . . in recognition of your very kind
service . . . I don't know how to pass the line . . . could you help
my friend . . . thank you, thank you, thank you, dear M.
Laporterie . . . dear Raoul . . . " They were from rich Parisians,
peasants from farms in Landes, doctors, soldiers, men, women,
children, Jews, nuns, priests, Freemasons, communists — all
the persecuted of Nazi Europe.

One came from his friend Mme Jeanne Lafaysse in Bordeaux.
She was the assistant manager of Dewachter, one of the major
clothing stores in the rue Ste-Catherine. The store was owned
by Léo Castel, and Laporterie bought cloth from him for the
La Petite Maison chain in Landes. Mme Lafaysse wanted to
know if Laporterie could help protect the Castels from the
anti-Semitic laws that the Germans were enforcing all over
Occupied France and that the Vichy French were imitating.
Léo, a Jew, was going to sell the store to her for safekeeping
while he and his wife's family, who were Christian, fled to . . .
where? That was the question Lafaysse posed.

Grenade in those days was a dull, genial town, where everyone traded with farmers. The place was enlivened mainly by
gossip on days of church *fêtes*, or commercial fairs, during the
summer days of the *corrida* and bull-jumping, but for weeks on
end in winter it was gray, cold, drizzling, whipped by winds
bearing the salty smell of the Atlantic a hundred kilometers
west. In summer it lay stunned by the heat, the gray walls
bleached by the dazzling sun, dust ballooning behind the idly

clacking wheels of the farm carts that rattled in from the plain to the north, or down the hill through the shadowy woods to the humped bridge over the Adour. There was one bridge, one church, one square, one language, one school, one bank. There was no château. There was no library.

Between houses and sidewalks there were no gardens; the windows gave directly out on the pedestrians, and in to the man inside with his glass of the local *madiran* wine, listening to the laughter of the girls walking by arm in arm. In winter, his window frames would rattle to the huge slam of the wind dragged behind the trucks hammering the pavement en route to Pau, on the edge of the Pyrénées 150 kilometers south. Gossip here spread as easily as the wood smoke from the chimneys over the close-packed houses. The people knew each other well, their ways and ideas; they forgot nothing; they did not like one to rise above the rest. The farm women came to town in winter, sockless in open sandals or clogs, the skin of their feet cracking from cold and exposure, and they did not like the shiny black leather on the neat uncallused feet of Monsieur le Maire Raoul Laporterie. He was *un grand monsieur*. He was growing too big for himself; he set others to do work for which he then reaped the credit. But many more forgave him his energy and his gifts. They followed his example — in their dress, in their entertainment, their insurance and, finally, at his behest, in risking their lives for people they understood only as *les Israélites*, the people of the Bible, the rag traders of Bordeaux, now inexplicably hunted by the Nazis. These Nazis also wanted to seize the French patriots who were continuing the resistance abandoned by the government. Thus there was suddenly a terrible conjunction of interest between the remains of proud France and the few Jews of the diaspora still alive in Bordeaux.

CHAPTER 2

Saving the People

IN JULY 1940, the German army moved in to Mont-de-Marsan to take over the air base and set up a control post on the new frontier line between Occupied France, to the northwest, and Vichy France. Germans in uniform soon arrived at Laporterie's store expecting to be served. The assistant store manager came up to Laporterie's dim little office for advice. Laporterie told him to simply treat the Germans like regular customers, then went downstairs himself to casually look around. He recognized one of the Germans, an officer who was in charge of passport and identity papers at the *préfecture*. Laporterie went up to him, shooing away the salesman in order to serve the officer himself. The German asked for a suit to be made in English worsted, a cloth that was unobtainable in Germany. Laporterie said with a smile, "You know that's very hard to get hold of these days. Why don't you go get it yourself? You know where it's made."

The officer stared at him in astonishment for a moment, then burst out laughing. "I will, M. Laporterie," he said, "I will. But first you will make a new uniform for my victory parade down Pall Mall? Agreed?"

"Agreed."

There was a road running through a shallow wooded valley to one side of the highway just south of Mont-de-Marsan. On his way to Bascons that afternoon, Laporterie saw a pair of gray vans parked, one on either side of it. Lumber was lying around, and French civilian workmen in blue were constructing a little control cabin while German soldiers in gray supervised. Laporterie slowed down, looking around. The vehicles belonged to the SS troops in Mont-de-Marsan. Right here between his home in Grenade and his main store in Mont-de-Marsan ran the demarcation line separating Occupied France, under Hitler, from the free zone, under Pétain at Vichy.

Laporterie stopped to ask about the line. The German officer in charge said there would be a neutral zone two kilometers wide beginning here. On the other side of the zone would be the post of the government of Vichy France. "Starting on Monday, everyone will have to have an *Ausweis* (pass)," said the officer. "Papers, please." He held out his hand. For a moment, torn between pride and need, Mayor Laporterie, *conseiller d'arrondissement*, victorious veteran of the First World War, hesitated. Then he drew out his leather case and showed the papers. The German waved him on.

Walking through Bascons, he met some of the refugees he had sheltered. "What do you think, Mister Mayor?" some of them asked him. "Are the Germans annexing Alsace? Lorraine, too? Will they let us go home?"

He had heard nothing official yet in Mont-de-Marsan, the capital of the *département* of Landes. He said he didn't know what the Germans were up to in the north, but he pointed out that there must be hope because "most of you are farmers, and the Boche need to eat, too, *hein?*"

He walked up the marble stairs of the Bascons town hall to his second-floor office. Again his mail was swollen with requests. What to do? he wondered, looking out the window that faced west over the hot dry fields. A warm wind blew gently through the open window, spicy with the smells of the fields. His secretary, M. Dumartin, a quiet, hardworking man, came in to tell him that the Vichy government had ordered the mayors of France to remove from their offices the signs and symbols of the former republic. They would be replaced with the new symbols of the Etat Français. The idealistic Liberty, Equality, Fraternity would be replaced by the insipid motto Family, Work, Country. Laporterie glanced up at the marble statue of the mythical symbol of France, Marianne. "Leave everything as it is," he said.

He went downstairs. The pavement radiated heat up into his face. Walking north along the street, empty now because everyone was home for dinner, he faced the immense south wall of the Romanesque church, which blocked off the end of the main street, giving a small part of Bascons the urban feel of walls towering over narrow streets. On top of the slanting stone caps of the buttresses grew bushes. Everything was worn by sun and wind. The date on the builder's stone, which had been set into the south side of the church six centuries earlier, was almost gone. Laporterie walked up the shallow stone front steps and stood looking out at the empty square before him down the slight slope clothed with wildflowers and grass to the creek, which he knew from his boyhood was by now shallow and warm. He could see the red-tile roof of the public well and washhouse, where every week all the women of the village, including his mother, scrubbed their clothes on the stone. A car drove along the road by the washhouse, pulling a cloud of white dust behind it. The mayor's side of his mind weighed the cost of calcium chloride to keep down the dust against the cost of paving a kilometer of road. He thought with pleasure of the pleasure of the women who would no longer have to suffer the dust. But almost certainly there would be no road improvements while the Germans were running France.

He walked around the church toward the graveyard. In ancient times, the attic of the church had been filled with grain when invasion threatened. People of the village had sheltered here, defending themselves with bows and arrows through the archers' slits beside the flat-fronted belfries. Everything Laporterie was had been formed here, by his parents, friends, priest, teachers, including his belief in the Christian teachings of his mother. He loved the story she told him of Saint Vincent de Paul, a young priest from a village near Dax, who freed slaves and built homes for children he had found abandoned in the streets of Paris. The young Raoul had imagined himself as the eloquent Vincent, persuading the king of France to liberate the slaves chained in his galleys. This was a role the mature Laporterie had already begun to live out when he helped to protect Spanish Republican refugees and the Alsatians.

The German occupation attacked the great ideals of the state that he believed in. The Germans were destroying liberty, enforcing inequality and replacing fraternity with hatred. The anti-Semitic laws of Nazi Germany were now being promulgated in the occupied zone: property was being confiscated, refugees were being deported to hideous work camps, the right to practice a profession was soon to be taken away. The generous Castel family sought his help, Mme Jeanne Lafaysse had told him. What could he do for them?

Men who resisted were rare in Landes in 1940. People of the region were old-fashioned, politically centrist, living with traditions that dated from feudal times. Landes was known as one of the most backward regions in France. In 1939, the land was still parceled out to many small farmers, making it impossible to shift to new crops, such as soybeans or corn, or to new techniques, such as tractors or manufactured fertilizers, because of the investment and education required. The villages had no public libraries. Schooling was perfunctory. To the Landais, friendship, family life and simple joys were what counted most; a man having an affair with a married woman might awake one morning to find a trail of white beans leading from his door to hers. In the village of Bascons, there were four automobiles among 400 people. These conservative, hospitable, cheerful, healthy, pragmatic people did not resist the

Germans in 1940 but accommodated themselves to their presence as they would to a drought.

Whatever Laporterie did to help the Castels meant risking his precious position in the community, because by protecting the Jews he would be defying the legitimate government of the heroic Pétain.

Helping Jewish refugees was, in that summer of 1940, not as dangerous as the Germans made it a few months later, because the Germans themselves were trying to dump foreign-born Jews over the demarcation line into Vichy France. But Vichy did not want either the foreign-born Jews or any increase in the number of refugees, who were already crowding out the natives. So there was that summer more game than danger in the "dangerous game," as Laporterie later called it. Still, he was moved to act when others weren't, to take time and trouble for refugees, simply because they needed his help. Thus, little by little at first, he was drawn into a struggle against Hitler over people's lives. Those whom the Germans saw only as Jews, Laporterie saw as people.

He was moved when others were not because he was angry at the persecution of innocent men, their wives and children and grandparents. They have no right to do this, he thought, listening to the stories of the Gestapo atrocities beginning in Paris. This is monstrous. Rage destroyed his doubt.

Passionately he wanted to fight the Germans, but prudently he looked for a safer way. In the garden of the house he had inherited from his parents here in Bascons, he had already buried twenty-four pistols against the day when the French would rise up against the Germans. But people were begging him for help now. What could he do? He looked around the graveyard, reading the names of the dead. He realized that the dead still had one thing that could solve the problem. Identity. All he had to do was resurrect the dead in order to save the living.

André Tachon, who worked in Laporterie's store in Mont-de-Marsan and lived in Grenade near Laporterie, knew from the moment he saw the maps that Laporterie would never accept the demarcation line. Tachon, a burly man with a friendly untroubled face, looked naive, but he was caustically cynical about the ruling classes to which Pétain and most of the men of Vichy belonged.

"I was disgusted from the moment I saw the call-up notices," Tachon told him. "You know why? Because it called us all for a service of twenty-one days. Imagine. Asking us to believe we would beat the Germans in twenty-one days. But we knew why. Because they didn't trust us to come for a month to save France. That's what they thought of us."

"Because they won't do anything for France themselves, they think no one else will," said Laporterie. "Alors, André, let's take an aperitif together."

It was unusual for a boss like Laporterie, owner of four stores in the region, a man with important political power, to make friends with a young employee. But Laporterie, who had no son, looked on young André with a fatherly affection. Always neat and organized himself, he was often irritated by dilatory, imprecise Tachon, and always forgave him. For a moment as they sat down outdoors in a café surveying the Place de la Poste, he hesitated, seeing Germans in uniform, Tachon's face. Could this youth, excitable, not well educated, inexperienced, carry out what lay ahead? Did André in fact feel as Laporterie felt? Would he see that Laporterie's plan was essential? Would he risk his life? Finally, did Raoul have the right to ask André to put his life at risk? In the end he decided not only that André had the goodwill, but another quality that was essential to the game he was going to play. He was as brave as a man could be. And he would be utterly loyal. Laporterie made up his mind. But first there was a question to settle.

"Alors, you have finished your military service, haven't you?" Laporterie asked.

"Yes, of course. Why?"

"So you can't be called up again. Listen, how would you like to help me resurrect the dead?" Laporterie said with a laugh.

"What are you talking about?"

"I'm getting all kinds of letters here and at Bascons asking me to help people find each other, or escape across the line, or pass mail. I have to do something. I need your help."

"What can I do?"

"When we get a request to pass someone across the line, we'll look up the records in Bascons, find someone with about the same birth date who is now dead or missing, and then we'll issue new papers in that name. You see? It's very simple. The refugees just take over the names of dead Basconnais."

"But the Germans will soon suspect."

"Why should they?"

"Well, all of a sudden a blond young man in flying boots with his arm in a sling who can't speak French is at the border alongside some Jews with Paris accents in fur coats and Worth dresses, all going home to their mothers in Bascons." He laughed. "Suppose the German says, 'Where is Bascons?' "

They both laughed. Laporterie said, "If we get a British pilot, we take him across unconscious in an ambulance. I was in an ambulance unit in the First World War, so I know the whole routine. The Paris Jews can be born again in Abbeville."

"What's so special about Abbeville?"

"The city hall was destroyed during the fighting. All the records were burned."

"Ah, that's good," said Tachon approvingly.

"What do you say? Shall we give it a try?" Laporterie's voice was excited, his alert blue eyes searching the square casually from time to time to see if everything looked normal. He looked hopefully at Tachon's big frank face.

"I would like to help you," said Tachon. "You know I'd follow you anywhere. But I think we must be very careful."

"I know. We'll be working without a net," said Laporterie. He wondered if this young man, who was infuriatingly late all the time, was hinting that he, Laporterie, was irresponsible.

Tachon said, "They're everywhere, even in the free zone."

"Listen, you see how I have built up my business," said Laporterie impatiently. "From nothing. I assure you, my mother did not push me here in a wheelbarrow."

"No, no, I admire what you've done in business, but this is not business. In business you must take risks, I know, but if we are going to pass people right under the Germans' beards, we have to do it like a cat jumping a bird."

"Gently, André," said Laporterie. "Is this like a cat or not?" He showed Tachon papers for a whole family from Bordeaux who were hoping to cross with him. The photographs were already attached, there were worn streaks across the paper and each one fitted perfectly into an old leather wallet.

Tachon sighed with relief. "Where did you get the wallets?"

"I asked around. It's absurd, I can make as many of these things as I like." He tapped the papers. "The hard thing is to get old wallets so it all looks authentic."

"We'll just have to collect them from the refugees."

"No, you don't understand. There won't be time. We won't even see these people until the day they arrive to cross. The papers won't look worn into the wallets."

"I meant they can donate their old wallets as they go by, then we have a supply for the next batch."

"Ah, yes, that's good."

Laporterie was glad to have Tachon beside him. Now when he crossed the line he joked with the lonely Germans, making them feel at home. He offered them suits cut from cloth of a quality they couldn't find in their own country. Once in a while he brought them a present. Soon they welcomed the sight of this jaunty good-humored man. Soon after that, they were sure of him. Once they were sure of him, he was sure of them.

As soon as the Wehrmacht took power in Paris, the Gestapo arrived, hunting down Jewish refugees from Germany and Eastern Europe. They smashed down doors to get at the refugees or their possessions. Men, women and children were deported to concentration camps in Germany. In Bordeaux, a Polish refugee boy named Israel Karp was shot by the Germans for shaking his fist at a tank during a German victory parade in August.

Karp's defying Hitler's armies was exactly what Hitler had planned. In the thirties, Hitler harassed the Jews to make them resist, so he could declare them enemies of the state. The Jews could then be crushed in place of the enemies Hitler could not yet reach — France, England and America, who had humiliated the Germans in 1918. Although he was now victorious abroad, Hitler still had enemies at home, whom he silenced with victories over Poland, France and Israel Karp. Next in line to Karp were the Jews of the rag trade along rue Ste-Catherine in Bordeaux — the Castels, Yaeches, Angels, as well as the Cassuttos, the Aboressys and people in other trades. Seeking to flee, they were at first confronted with a bizarre difficulty. These were the months the Germans were preparing to deport German refugees to camps in the east, and shoving other Jews out of Occupied France into the Vichy zone. But Pétain's government, betraying the generosity of the French Republic, vigorously opposed the German dumping program. Early in October 1940, Vichy announced new repressive measures against enemies of the state, mainly Jews, as if to mollify the Germans. Along with the Jews, Vichy named "parliamentarians and Freemasons." It is one of the oddest ironies of Pétain's quirky regime that in this set of measures designed to purify France of its enemies, there is no mention of the enemies occupying sixty percent of the country. Only the defenseless were attacked, in a chilly echoing of Hitler's words about his policy toward Jews in Germany: "Once the hatred and the battle against the Jews have been really stirred up, their resistance will necessarily crumble. . . . They are totally defenseless and no one will stand up to protect them."[1]

Vichy's anti-Semitism momentarily bewildered French Jewish citizens in the summer of 1940: would they be worse off under the plainly anti-Semitic laws of the German regime in the north, compounded by Vichy's civil laws,[2] or could they find refuge farther from Germany in Vichy France, despite the emerging anti-Semitism of that regime?

Their doubts were soon resolved by ordinances on the German side. In the regions, beginning that autumn, local ordinances followed the general German line, which originated in Berlin. The police of Bordeaux were among the first to pass local ordinances against Jews. The initial repressive measures, aimed at communists and foreigners, were arranged by the head of the Bordeaux police, Special Commissioner Fredon, with his new German counterpart, Commandant Hortman. The repression organized by the Germans and Vichy in the area soon extended to Freemasons, Jews, Gypsies and others.

The Sephardic Jews of Bordeaux were worried by the influx of the strange Ashkenazi Jews, whom they called "far-distant relatives."[3] These foreigners, in flight from Germany, Poland, Czechoslovakia and Austria, practiced a different liturgy and spoke with foreign accents. The Bordeaux Sephardim, numbering only about 3000 in 1939, were themselves descended from refugees, who had been chased out of Spain and Portugal in the fifteenth and sixteenth centuries.

Aware of distinctions among various Jews, the Nazis considered for a while the possibility of excepting the Sephardim from the fires to come. The German police commander in Bordeaux said this was because "from the point of view of race, they are not to be considered Jews at all. The Sephardim call themselves Latin Spaniards of the Mosaic rite. I ask you to give me a short report on the Sephardim living in the Gironde [region of Bordeaux], their number, the police view of their political situation, and if up till now they have been excepted in individual cases. . . ."⁴

Nissim Yaeche, who owned a fabric store in Bordeaux, had seen disaster coming from far away. The first sign was Kristallnacht, on the night of November 9, 1938, when the Nazis first attacked Jews openly in Germany; the next was the betrayal of Czechoslovakia by Britain and France, then their refusal to fight until the Germans attacked in 1940. The murder of Israel Karp, the warning closest to home, was soon followed by another. Pierre Mourgues, of Bordeaux, who said that he could not be charged with harboring a prostitute who had contaminated the Germans because "pigs cannot be contaminated," was shot by the humorless Germans in December 1940.⁵

Yaeche thought of fleeing with his wife, Sarah, and their three children, but he stayed. He couldn't get much for the business he had built through the depression, and so he would have only his meager savings for support if he left Bordeaux. His parents-in-law, living above his store on the rue Ste-Catherine, didn't believe they were in any danger, because they were Greek citizens under the protection of the Greek government. Yaeche, a considerate, thoughtful man, didn't like to press them, so he delayed acting even after the government fled from Paris to Bordeaux, along with thousands of refugees from central Europe.

Yaeche believed that his family, too, must flee, but he couldn't bring himself to act. He didn't want to abandon his wife's parents. He didn't know where he could take them. He didn't see what good it would do to flee, because the Germans could hunt down on the shores of the Atlantic a refugee like Karp who had come from the borders of Russia. He didn't want to flee in poverty to an alien country where he would be ignorant of the language. He didn't see the use of fleeing anywhere in France without false papers, and he didn't know how to get false papers.

His mind was made up for him one Friday evening by the president of the Bordeaux Chamber of Commerce, who came to his store. "The Germans have just decided that Jews can't own businesses any longer," he told Yaeche. "You'll have to sell."

"When?" said Yaeche, who was not surprised.

"Before Monday." Now he was surprised. He had only two days, both Sabbaths — Jewish and Christian — to do his business.

The next morning a local furrier, M. Gamberto, who had heard the news, came to make an offer. He said he sympathized with Yaeche's problem because his own wife and parents-in-law were Jewish. But he told Yaeche that he could leave without worrying. "I'll take care of it for you," he said. "I'll send you a share of the profits every month, and when you come back, I'll give it back to you just as I found it today." As Yaeche's daughter, Huguette, said, "My father had a knife to his throat. What else could he do but accept?" He went upstairs to tell Sarah's parents the news, but they refused to leave. Courteously he argued with them. "How can the Greek government protect you here?" he asked. "What does Hitler care for international agreements. What will you do if he invades Greece? He is here now. We have to get away."

"We're old. God will protect us," they said.

"Let Him protect you in the free zone, then," said Yaeche.

"Why would the Nazis bother with a couple of old people like us?"

They refused to budge.

Yaeche went across the street to see Mme Jeanne Lafaysse, the cheerful, determined woman who now owned and operated Léo Castel's store. She told Yaeche that Raoul Laporterie, who had brought the Castels safely into Vichy France, would take him across the line anytime he wanted.

"What about my wife and children?" He had three children, Huguette, fourteen, Albert, ten, and Roger, five.

Mme Lafaysse said they could all come. M. Laporterie would take care of everything.

"And how much will this cost?" Yaeche asked.

"Nothing."

"Nothing? But he must have expenses. He must spend a lot of time on this."

"He accepts the costs."

Yaeche told his wife that they would be leaving in a few days. In the car that M. Laporterie was sending, there would be room for only one small suitcase each, so most of the bags would have to cross later. New photographs were taken for false identity papers Laporterie would supply. They all helped to carry up to the apartment above the store the most valuable merchandise, to hide it in hopes that their exile would be brief. The furrier Gamberto himself said he hoped they would come back soon, unharmed. He promised to send them part of the profits every month so they would have something to live on. Yaeche did not mention that he had a small stock of gold *louis d'or* coins, which he had been building up ever since he saw the first signs of the pogrom beginning in Germany.

"Where will we go?" his wife asked as they packed bags in their small apartment, which was crowded with furniture.

"I don't know. Perhaps to Limoges." He had sent a letter to his brother-in-law, Elie Safaty, who lived there; it had gone secretly via Laporterie, because the Germans were permitting only postcards with preprinted messages to cross. Yaeche was also hoping to get visas so they could all escape to Algeria, perhaps even eventually to North America.

Laporterie drove down alone from Mont-de-Marsan in the Juvaquatre to pick up the family. He took them to a little flat in Mont-de-Marsan that he had borrowed for the night from a friend. They were all nervous. That night, Huguette Yaeche had nightmares about the crossing the next day. Yaeche, too, must have had serious doubts about the wisdom of running away. Mont-de-Marsan, which was just inside the occupied zone, had looked so normal that fleeing seemed bizarre. Like Sarah's parents, most French people didn't believe the hideous rumors coming out of Germany about the concentration camps. To escape a danger that might be imaginary, Nissim Yaeche was committing infractions that certainly put him in real danger. If he was caught, he would be convicted of smuggling gold under a false name, of illegal entry, using false papers. He would certainly be deported, along with Sarah and the children.

Laporterie arrived early the next day, smiling confidently, papers all arranged. He told them they could stay in his own second house in Bascons for as long as they liked. The sensitive Huguette immediately fell in love with this charming man, who treated her mother and father with such courtesy while risking his life for them. She adored his beautiful blue eyes, his skinny mustache, his elegant suit, his eau de cologne, his complexion glowing like a baby's, his smile, his certainty. She felt absolutely safe with him. Forty years later, still charmed, she believed that most women adored him as she did.

She listened to Laporterie telling her father that for today the family would be divided. Nissim Yaeche was reborn on a new identity card as Jean Laffont, merchant, of Bascons, complete with Ausweis, printed in German, permitting him to cross the frontier once, today. The papers were completely authentic; they were those of the Jean Laffont who had been born, baptized — and buried — in Bascons.

Sarah Yaeche became Laure Laporterie, so Huguette became Laporterie's daughter for the day. She was shyly pleased, but Yaeche and Sarah were vaguely embarrassed by this hoax. They were entrusting themselves to this blue-eyed stranger, whose rakish mustache and well-tailored suit seemed, to the conservative Yaeches, suspiciously dapper. Was this Laporterie simply a foolish fop who would fumble them into the hands of the Gestapo? Was he a pretty crook who, in the middle of the passage, would suddenly stop to demand a huge payment? The bones of refugees abandoned by thieving *passeurs* were already bleaching in the trails of the high Pyrénées.

Laporterie had already told him that they shouldn't take anything valuable along with them in case they were searched. Yaeche had to give Laporterie all Sarah's jewels together with all his *louis d'or* coins. Later, when Laporterie was crossing alone so that the car would not be searched, he would bring the gold and jewels across the line.

They stopped at the striped barrier. Two Wehrmacht guards approached the car, ordering them all out. They greeted Laporterie amiably, but ordered "Laffont" into the guardhouse, where they questioned him and checked his identity card, ration card and *Ausweis* against each other and against his appearance. They looked through the car, finding nothing incriminating. "Mme Laporterie," her son and two daughters passed without problems. Laporterie joked and smoked with them as the searches were going on, then they were back in the car, safely heading for the Vichy post two kilometers ahead. The guards gave Laporterie, Madame and their passengers only a perfunctory check, for Laporterie was a mayor in a tailored suit with impeccable credentials.

He took them to the house he had grown up in at Bascons. The village, like many in the south of France, grew magically during the war. The population of about 450 apparently rose in a year to more than 1850, as Laporterie, in effect, emptied the graveyard back into the village. At that point he expanded to another graveyard in another village near Bordeaux, where a friendly secretary gave him more names to use.

The Lafonts-Laporteries moved in under their own name. Laporterie felt this was safer because at this stage of the war no one in Bascons would betray them, nor did it seem likely that the Gestapo or Vichy police would make a raid. Mme Yaeche caused a sensation in Bascons during the winter by wearing her beautiful fur coat. Many records for cold were set that winter, so she was often seen in the coat in the village. One day a village housewife said to her that she really shouldn't use such a fine coat for everyday wear in Bascons. Mme Yaeche said, "But it's all I have."

At this point, Laporterie's system of passing — getting people across the demarcation line — was based on the use and reuse of a pool of thirty or forty passes, including Laure's, which gave him enough options in age, sex, color of hair, eyes and complexion, to cover all cases. To issue permanent identity cards was more difficult, so he didn't bother at first. Vichy's pursuit of communists, Jews and downed flyers from the north was not yet organized, so the Yaeches were able to live under their own names for the months they spent in the village.

As the official xenophobia in Vichy rose, so did the compassion of the ordinary French people for the victims. All over France people began to unite to help anyone pursued by the Nazis of Vichy or Berlin. In Le Chambon-sur-Lignon, high in the mountains southwest of Lyon, Protestant villagers, raised in a religion long persecuted in France, continued taking in refugees as they had been doing since the early thirties. The refugees at first were Spanish Republicans, then Eastern Europeans fleeing from Hitler, now all kinds of Jews fleeing both Hitler and Vichy. More than 5000 refugees came to Le Chambon during the war. All of them were saved by the Chambonnais and their Catholic neighbors, who later joined in. To this day, no one in Catholic Bascons has even heard of Protestant Le Chambon, yet in both villages the reaction to the persecution of the refugees was exactly the same: to help them regardless of the risk.

Germaine Gourdon, Laporterie's cousin, a strong, merry woman who ran the bakery, used to go around in a horse and buggy to the small mills in the countryside collecting a little flour to bring back to Bascons for the refugees. The actual population rose from about 450 to around 600 at its peak, all the extras being refugees. Some of these people had no ration cards for a while, but she had taken it upon herself to feed them somehow. When people lined up to buy bread from her in the morning, she didn't open the door or the hungry people would rush in without lining up. She sold the bread through the window, often to people who had no ration cards, on the basis of need. At night she would help her husband, who was first assistant in the *mairie* (mayor's office) to make false identity cards with Laporterie.

Huguette Yaeche loved to see Raoul Laporterie's small energetic figure approaching, because he was like a ray of sunshine in their lives. He brought over the gold and jewels safely, money arrived from Gamberto, and the Yaeches were able to enjoy life again in Bascons. Laporterie gave Yaeche a bicycle and taught him to ride it. Yaeche was not well coordinated, so he was sometimes cut and bruised when he arrived at Laporterie's store in Grenade. In the second-floor kitchen they would talk while Laure cooked and listened to them, or mended clothes. At 9:20 P.M. they all listened to the BBC.

CHAPTER **3**

Growing Up Landais

Y AECHE AND Laporterie, sitting in the
Laporteries' salon listening to the radio through enemy jam-
ming, were living an era uncannily like the Cold War years.
Their country was impoverished, and their people frightened
by threats of war, yet the country was not at war. Their country
was not at war, but they were both in immediate danger of
violent death. They had been betrayed by their leaders. Their
government ruled by fear and lies. They had been free but now
they moved like spies in their own country. Their leaders could
not defend the country by arms because they feared far greater
violence in retaliation. Their country was in danger of extinc-
tion. There was no protection against their enemies.

This was an unimaginable state when Laporterie was born,
on August 13, 1897, in the same bed where he now slept with
his wife. Bascons in 1897 was a calm little place where people
lived close to one another and knew a lot about one another.
The Landais are hospitable people who don't leave a visitor on
the doorstep. They love to eat and drink well, but they don't
worry about money, either lacking it or getting it. In recent
times what has been developed there are not medicines, inven-
tions, art or philosophy, but the style of cooking at the heart
of modern French cuisine. The Landais and their neighboring
cousins have given the world Armagnac, Landais bull-dancing,

the best *foie gras* in the world and a very large bank, the Crédit Agricole.

Raoul Laporterie, a busy, gregarious boy, was always mature for his age. He soon knew all the children and most of the adults of Bascons. For days, perhaps weeks at a time, he never saw a face he did not know. The children he led, the adults he charmed. The most exciting events of his year were the *fêtes* and bullfights. Every summer there were *fêtes* in Grenade and Mont-de-Marsan and bullfights in Mont-de-Marsan. At Bascons, there was also the Course Landaise, a modern form of bull-dancing.

The bull, or an aggressive young cow, is led into the ring, tethered by one of its long, sharp horns. The young *sauteur* (dancer) faces the charging animal without cape, sword or the help of a picador. As the half-ton animal is about to hit him at about forty kilometers an hour, the *sauteur* leaps into the air, the animal charges underneath, stops in a swirl of dust, then charges again. The man leaps again, to dive over the bull's back, or bounce off it, or twirl in the air like a diver, in maneuvers that seem unchanged from the bull-dancing painted on the frescoes and vases of Minoan Crete 3500 years ago. This daring, usually bloodless, encounter thrilled young Raoul, but it lasted only a few hours a year.

Early in his life, Raoul began helping his father and mother in the store when he was not at the village school. He was happy with his mother, whom he adored. To him she was simply a saint who radiated loving kindness. She was very popular among her neighbors because she extended credit to them easily, without pestering them about repayment. His father, a handsome, charming man, cut a dashing figure even in Mont-de-Marsan. He had been born in Mont-de-Marsan, where he became musical director of the local brass band, which marched through the *fêtes* and bullfights in gorgeous red-and-white uniforms loudly playing red-and-white band music. Raoul doted on and dominated his brother, Jean-Marie, who was two years younger.

Everyone in the village spoke Gascon, the local patois, but school was conducted in proper French, so Raoul soon realized that there was a huge difference between his home and the much greater world outside, which the books on his school desk revealed.

The education was trivia taught by rote, enforced by punishment. He craved to get out of little Bascons. The smell of the salt of the sea in the foggy air of morning made him dream of Bordeaux. The tourists on the trains to Pau, a small city to the southwest, made him imagine the huge stations in Paris. On the plateau above Grenade he pumped his bicycle straight toward the horizon he loved, barbed with the peaks of the Pyrénées in Spain.

Raoul lived for a time in Mont-de-Marsan with his grandparents, going to school near the arena. He loved the bullfights, so he hung around the arena, occasionally getting work as an usher. During the actual fights, the ushers sat on the cement steps between the paying customers, shouting their approval or whistling their distaste.

After a couple of years, his parents sent him to board at Aire-sur-l'Adour, an energetic little city halfway to Pau, which was a fashionable spa for the English rich. When Raoul was seventeen his father left to fight in the First World War, and Raoul was called back to Bascons to help his mother.

He spent two and a half years there learning the trade that became his livelihood. He was glad to be close once more to his beloved mother, but Bascons was now for him impossibly small. In 1916, he enlisted, received a quick training, then visited his father briefly at the front before he went into the line himself.

Two stiff-necked generals, the German von Falkenhayn and the peasant Frenchman Pétain, who had already led millions of young men to slaughter, were now preparing for the holocaust of Verdun, in northeast France. Both Laporteries were flung into the hideous battle. Both survived the butchery of almost a million young men in a few months. Afterward, von Falkenhayn was removed from command, but Pétain became a hero, even to Laporterie.

Unlike the intensely loyal Laporterie, by 1917 many of the French soldiers, sickened by the massacre, were mutinous. Pétain, now known as the Hero of Verdun and the Savior of France, restored order by responding to their complaints of bad food and favoritism to the officers. The war continued as before.

Laporterie, with most of his battalion, was captured on June 9, 1918, during General Ludendorff's last offensive. He was crowded into a cattle car with dozens of other men. They were without food and water all night as the train rolled slowly eastward. East of Aix-la-Chapelle in the morning, when the exhausted prisoners opened a trapdoor in the roof for air, the German civilians threw stones at them.

In the prison camp, Laporterie came down with an abscessed tooth. A doctor extracted it without an anesthetic while the young man clutched at the wooden packing case on which he was sitting. His mouth was rinsed out with water he had already been told was unfit to drink. Influenza killed prisoners and guards throughout the camps.

He recovered, weak and thin, but no longer in danger of death, to be sent to Bremen on the north coast of Germany. In Bremen, the prisoners slowly starved. (Germany, blockaded by the Royal Navy, was so short of food that 763,000 civilians died from starvation.)[1]

Laporterie and others dug a tunnel under the camp courtyard — not to escape but to get at a silo full of potatoes that stood in a far corner of the yard. The stolen potatoes, which they managed to cook secretly at night, probably saved their lives.

Each day they were forced to work long hours side by side

with German workmen in an adjacent factory. The prisoners helped to make submarines to sink the ships bringing them the hope of freedom from Canada and the United States. The German boy working beside Laporterie felt sorry for his French partner. Despite the fact that the boy's father had been killed in the war he was not bitter toward the French. One day, to Laporterie's amazement, he invited him home for dinner. The boy sneaked his father's suit into the factory past the guards for Laporterie to wear, and Laporterie walked out of the factory one evening beside him. They went to the boy's house where the weakened Laporterie restored himself with the best meal he had eaten in months, although, as he told the other prisoners later, "the coffee was terrible." After dinner, the boy escorted him back to the factory where he sneaked in by mingling with the night shift of civilians.

Another German in the factory, this one from Alsace, befriended Laporterie. The man, whispering in German-spattered French hard for Laporterie to understand, offered to help him escape. Laporterie said he would not go alone. The Alsatian said there would be seven Frenchmen and nine Belgians going. Laporterie accepted.

The Alsatian got them all civilian clothes. They went over the wall at night, ran to a railway line leading west and started walking. They managed to hitch a ride on a slow freight for a while, then jumped off and kept on walking west on the tracks, hoping to reach neutral Holland eighty kilometers to the west.

One morning on a back road they were stopped by a river with no bridge. One of the escapees noticed German soldiers in the distance, so they hid. They had been spotted by one German, who was wearing a red star on his cap. He came over to them peaceably. He told them not to worry about his uniform because the revolution had begun, so they were free. (Many Germans at this time foresaw a Communist revolution.) The Germans were all planning to flee to neutral Holland across the river. They had been standing around only because some of them were not quite ready to make the literal final plunge.

The escapees started down the bank. Now more armed Germans appeared, these ones still loyal to the kaiser, who was himself soon to desert to Holland. As Laporterie plunged into the water with the others, one of the loyal Germans shot an escapee. Laporterie and the others scrambled up the far bank unharmed and hid.

The Dutch people took them to an army barracks where they were well fed. In the showers, they rid themselves of the body lice that had infested them for months in their camp. Laporterie sent postcards to his mother and to his beautiful fiancée, Laure Guilhem. Then he rejoined his unit.

His father's band played "La Marseillaise" when the French soldiers returned in victory, then swung through the streets of Mont-de-Marsan in a parade, blasting out the loud brassy Spanish-style music the Landais love. Laporterie's war experiences had not made him a pacifist, but his patriotic ardor was stilled by the knowledge that the greatest change in France wrought by the war was that throughout the country many children had only a picture for a father.

On July 3, 1919, Laure Guilhem married Raoul Laporterie in Grenade. She was a sweet-natured, determined young woman who was devoted to Raoul. He was not only charming but also a war hero, because of his escape from the German prison camp.

Raoul wanted to work for himself, so with a little help from Laure's mother, the two started a business together. They bought two horses, a merchandise wagon, a stock of suits, dresses and cloth, and sheepskins for the warm jackets the Landais call *canadiennes*, then set out early every morning to sell in the neighboring villages.

All about Grenade were hamlets, villages, little towns, which had grown up mainly from medieval clusters of farm buildings. They were laced together by muddy earth roads probably first traced out in the times of the Celts. On the road from Grenade to Eugénie-les-Bains today stands a Celtic marker, or menhir, at least 3000 years old, eight feet high, inscribed with runes. It was a hard life at first on those roads for the young couple. They were up at six o'clock every morning to feed and harness the horses for the long day ahead. In every village they visited on the sandy pine-covered plain northeast of the Adour river, or on the valleyed plateau high above the river to the southwest and overlooked by the Pyrénées, stonecutters were incising the names of Landes's share of the ten million dead on cenotaphs under the motto *Mort pour la Patrie* or *Mort pour la France*.

Ah, tous ces braves gens, Laporterie thought wistfully as he saw the familiar family names over and over in Renung, Eugénie-les-Bains, Duhort-Bachen, Bascons, Bostens, Bretagne-de-Marsan, St-Maurice, Fargue, Montgaillard and Classun.

In 1920, Laure became pregnant. Their daughter, Irène, was born in 1921. She was a healthy child, blond, blue-eyed, resembling her father.

Right after the war plague swept over the Western world. In addition to the ten million people felled by war, at least ten million more died of Spanish influenza. Whenever Raoul and Laure had to get down from their wagon to help the horses get it up the muddy hill at Eugénie-les-Bains, they were pushing a weight of poverty and sorrow grown heavier with stupid politics. The young men of France had not lived to pave this road or build the truck that would ease the labor of Laure, Raoul and the rest of the working poor.

Laporterie thought about these things as they trundled out with their stock every day, wondering how to fix these politics, as well as how to make a better life for himself and Laure. The very look of the land they rode through was still medieval, parceled out in tiny lots, many less than one hectare (about two and one-half acres), which were completely unsuited to modern methods. Landes was known as one of the most backward *départements* of France. Here still survived the ancient system of *métayers* — workers, tenant farmers who resembled the serfs or land-bound peasants of medieval times. These *métayers* were barely educated, expected to live out their lives in loyal service to their semifeudal masters, not wander off to the cities in search of a better life. They were also expected to lay down their lives in defense of a system that enriched the leisure classes. Thus the very face of the land displayed the structure of society: small holdings intensively cultivated for sustenance crops, not for cash. Each château or big farm was close to self-sufficiency, producing not for the trade that spreads wealth, but only to protect the landowner's independence. Each cultivated the vine for wine; pigs, geese, ducks, chickens for the table; feed crops for the draft animals; fruit and vegetables for the table; wood for heat; some grains, even a little rice in a few paddies by the Adour. So the Laporteries sometimes had to barter their cloth for food, because in the beginning cash was so scarce.

The ignorant poverty of rural France pained Raoul deeply because he knew he, too, had its symptoms. He had gone to war thinking of himself as a "little guy" from a humble village, so he felt keenly the frustration of his inadequate French as he was argued down by glib men no smarter than he was. "I'm disgusted by all the mistakes I make when I speak and write," he told Laure. "I'm going to do something about it."

He read books and newspapers, cultivated the friendship of journalists like Georges Dubos of Mont-de-Marsan , a reporter on the big newspaper *Le Sud-Ouest*. He went to political rallies to hear notable speakers, practiced his handwriting so that the very formation of his words on paper was as clear as the thought he wanted to convey. He would also have to educate himself about politics and France. Finally he would have to increase his business so that he would have enough money and time to support his politics.

Laporterie was passionately indignant at the socialist argument that his generation had made their sacrifices in vain. Having offered his life to defend France, he could not bear to think that patriotism was, as the left said, an opiate like religion, used by the rich to divert the masses from the bourgeois enemy. He stuck to his arguments against the communists, but he had seen for himself during the war the injustice of the French capitalist system. Progress in education and technology seemed to him vital if the young Landais were to escape from ignorance and poverty like the Canadian and American farm boys who had fought beside him in the trenches. These men had towered over him, making him wonder about how they lived, how they had been fed at home. They had superb equipment, excellent horses and terrifying tanks that smashed relentlessly through the German barbed wire and trenches.

The crawling monsters that had helped the Allies win the war had advanced the technology of internal-combustion engines and traction so much that tractors were now common all over northern France. Yet there were in Landes no tractors, very few internal-combustion engines at all.

The life of the itinerant suited Laporterie's ebullient personality, as well as his ambition. He loved meeting people. Arriving in the tightly packed little villages with their houses leaning against each other like heads joined in conversation, he greeted people while the wagon was still rolling. A small nimble man, he would jump down lightly, smiling, offering his hand or a kiss, and listen. He was interested in everything — business, politics, family gossip, the crops, education. For Madame X he would bring a clipping from *Le Figaro* about Djibouti, where her son was serving in the navy; for Monsieur Y, a government report describing the wonders of some new crop — corn or soybeans — with instructions about planting. He was immensely popular, Laure was sympathetic, diligent and beautiful, so they were welcome on arrival, and the business thrived.

The widowed of the region had traditionally been taken care of by their children, so the many middle-aged parents who had lost sons in the war had also lost the assurance of support if one of them was incapacitated. Laporterie began to sell life insurance to people who had never heard of it before. As with most busy people, Laporterie found that time expands to accommodate work. He decided to take a night job managing the movie theater in Mont-de-Marsan. This was fun, it was new, he was entertained free, he met people and it put a little more money in his account at the Crédit Agricole. With a little help from his mother-in-law he set up the first movie theater in Grenade, where he was proprietor, manager and sometimes ticket seller. This was a big success, which pleased Laporterie, but not very lucrative, which didn't bother him.

He bought his first truck, a twenty-two-horsepower GMC, in the mid-twenties. Europeans were finally succeeding in reorganizing their economies. In France, production of cars and trucks rose year after year. The ancient animal paths could now be straightened out and paved. The new roads were especially important in the northern plain of Landes running toward the sea and in the ancient city of Bordeaux. People whose ancestors had lived out their whole lives in one *petit pays*, or small corner, where they were never more than thirty kilometers from their birthplace, could now criss-cross in a day that *petit pays*. They could afford to go to Bordeaux, light their houses at night, send the children to school for an extra year or three.

Laporterie soon saw that the new prosperity was going to change merchandising throughout Landes. The roads he and Laure used to reach the villagers would very soon be conveying them by car to town markets. The itinerant merchants with their market days shifting from village to village were doomed to disappear because the stores in the towns would suck up the trade. As people lived more sociably, style would become more important.

He and Laure began to expand their operation from a single

store in Grenade into the region. They opened in Mont-de-Marsan, then a branch in Hagetmau, to the southwest, then another in Mont-de-Marsan. Laporterie invested in excellence: he took pride in the modern design of the big new store in Mont-de-Marsan, he advertised a good deal, he laid in the best stock that the town had ever seen. The business did well despite the depression.

By the mid-thirties, Laporterie was probably better known in the Grenade region of Landes than was the premier of France, who, after all, changed every few months, while Laporterie continued. He was elected president of the Saint-Vincent-de-Paul Society of Bascons in January 1933, he founded or joined societies to promote bullfighting in Mont-de-Marsan or to bring back the Course Landaise to the region, he could be counted on to help in a drive to stamp out bovine tuberculosis, or to restore a crumbling church. Whatever he joined, he was almost always a vice president or president. He stood for municipal councillor in 1934 in Bascons and won, then for mayor of Bascons in 1935 and won, then for regional council in 1936 and won. Wearing the ribbons of seven medals from the First World War, he led the Grenade branch of the war veterans' association. He spoke at banquets, founded an arena, took the progressive side in all kinds of local issues. Whenever there was a meeting of a society that was ready to boost something in the neighborhood, Laporterie was more often than not in the room, welcomed by all, offering sound advice, as well as work. Every time he stood for office, he was elected.

Virtually all these societies were run by men, who were also the only members. Politics was masculine: women did not even have the vote in France, although women like Laure and her mother did much of the work. They were not embittered by their exploited or inferior status. They accepted it as the traditional norm, but they also saw that many of the Midi men were childish. Without the company of women they drank too much, put too high a value on violent sports such as rugby or bullfighting, drove their cars like toreadors, boasted to one another, or grew sentimental over macho symbols such as flags or a pair of bull's ears dripping blood. Drinking, like bullfighting or fast driving, was a bravura act to show that too much was not too much. All this bravado tended to make them incompetent, so the women often took over, quietly. French peasant women of the time often referred to their husbands as "my lodger," because the men paid so little attention to their wives — although they defended fiercely the idea of the family. Anywhere in France, but especially in Landes, it is easy to find a small business run by a competent woman whose man is drunk or asleep or traveling somewhere, or just sitting vacantly in a chair in the sun.

Laporterie, though he fitted without a crease into the male-dominated society, liked women without condescending to them. He ruled his house like a typical Landais male. But he was indulgently fond of Laure and her very capable mother and of Irène, who by the mid-thirties was a blue-eyed charmer like her father. Laporterie expected to be indulged at home, which meant that he was. When he returned home from traveling, or a night out, he did not expect to be questioned. There were no questions.

His friendships with other women were discreet. He maintained like a true Landais that the family was sacrosanct and that divorce was a serious mistake. Children must be acknowledged and protected by both parents. If a wife challenged her husband's freedom, she risked a beating. A saying of the day, repeated half a century later, was "Beat your wife every day; if you don't know why you're doing it, she does." Most men in Laporterie's part of the country in the 1930s believed all this.

The universe changes, France remains. So thought Laporterie and most of the French politicians of his time as they were building the Maginot line. "A Frenchman always thinks more or less of France as a Kosmos in the midst of a vast formless violent universe. The universe is convulsed, huge storms blow over it, but this does not affect the Kosmos."[2] In these words, Jean-Paul Sartre (in his memoirs of the opening months of the war) expressed an idea that grew to have a paralyzing effect on his country. Like a headache that presages a storm, the first few refugees began crowding into the Kosmos in the mid-thirties, first from Eastern Europe, then from Spain. A few friends of Laporterie's, whom he had met at bullfights in Madrid, fled from the fighting that broke out between fascist rebels under General Franco, supported by Germany and Italy, and the Republican government, supported officially by Russia, unofficially by volunteers from England, Canada, France and the United States. Several of the Republican Spaniards who had crossed the frontier without visas, or who wanted to stay in France after their visas ran out, were now interned at a French government camp in Gurs, near Pau. They wrote to Laporterie asking for help. Laporterie got them out because they were his friends, not because he sympathized with their socialist politics.

Socialism, in fact, angered him. It was weakening France, and communism was threatening the whole of Europe, Laporterie argued. He agreed with the politics of his friend Dr. Robert Bezos, of Mont-de-Marsan, who was the Radical Socialist member for Mont-de-Marsan in the Chambre des Députés (National Assembly) in Paris. The steep faults fissuring the French political system were apparent in the misleading name of Laporterie's party, which in fact stood firmly for centrist views. The lazy Bezos, sending Laporterie to do his job for him, typified the insoluble problems that Laporterie faced when he walked up the stairs of the métro station beside the Chambre des Députés building on the Boulevard St-Germain in Paris. As another patriotic observer of the government at that time wrote: "I saw men of incontestable value . . . come to the ministries. But the political game consumed them. . . . scarcely had a premier taken office than he was at grips with innumerable demands, criticisms and bids for favor, which all his energy was absorbed in warding off without ever contriving to master them. Parliament, far from supporting him, offered him nothing but desertions and ambushes. . . . Everyone knew he was there only for a few months."

Chaos entered Kosmos by the head. "The army," wrote the patriotic observer Charles de Gaulle, "which received from the state no more than spasmodic and contradictory impulses, was wedded to errors that had once constituted its glory. . . . " To him "it seemed deplorable to make the country believe that war, if it came, ought to consist, for it, in fighting as little as possible."[3]

France, beyond warning, was therefore beyond saving, like a cancer patient who continues to smoke. Very few people, despite de Gaulle, saw what was about to happen.

Laporterie was as delighted as a boy to be entrusted with plans, stamped Secret, for the mobilization of the French army in 1939. He also had with him plans for the evacuation of hundreds of thousands of Alsatians from their homes, because Alsace was again in the danger it had faced for centuries: of being the site as well as part of the cause for battle between the Frank and the Hun.

The French and the British who had made war inevitable by trying to avoid it were therefore not ready to fight when war came. The tanks sat. The planes did not fly. Nothing shot. Hitler took Poland while France and Britain did nothing.

The French government did, however, order the Alsatians to leave their villages two days after the declaration of war on September 3, 1939. There was little time for the refugees to lock up their farms and gather clothes, money, food, bedding, utensils. They had to leave the beasts in the pastures or the barns and the crops standing in the fields. As Curé Luttenbacher of Bartenheim said, "The exodus began miserably. Many hundreds of us were on the road, old, young, in whole families. We left in uncertainty, as if in night and fog. I can still see one brave woman, walking beside her cow, pulling at her wagon, to join me at the chapel for prayers before leaving."[4]

They slept in barns. The French troops passed them on the way to the front, waved cheerfully at them, and looted their locked houses.[5] "Fifteen days later," Curé Luttenbacher continues, "a train is leading us far, very far, too far, as far as possible. My section of the train finally heard our destination. Bascons." Within a few hours of receiving the name of their destination, they were informed by the refugee authorities that because of an error in planning they were not going to Bascons. "Where are we going?" they asked, but the commissioner had to tell them that there was no room for them. Yet, when they arrived at Mont-de-Marsan, everything was arranged again, and Laporterie was on the platform to welcome them.

Mayor René Kielwasser of Bartenheim was deeply touched by the warmth of Laporterie's greeting. "Spontaneously he offered to me shelter for all our families in his community. This beautiful unexpected gesture was a huge relief for all our hard-pressed refugees."[6]

Within three days, the senior Alsatians were back on the speaker's platform with the whole council of Bascons, while Laporterie made a farewell speech to the fathers and sons of the village as they were leaving for the front. "For all Basconnais in arms, for everyone who is leaving tomorrow, to you, women and children and old people who must remain, I say *courage* and *au revoir*."

CHAPTER 4

Anarchist in Office

WHILE HITLER, Pétain and de Gaulle con-
tended for the right to rule him, Laporterie became his own
government. He decided to do what he wanted, regardless of
Vichy or Hitler. While carrying out some of the laws of Vichy
in his offices as mayor or *conseiller d'arrondissement*, or obeying
other laws in daily life, he was also secretly breaking some, in
line with de Gaulle's call to resistance. Sometimes he had only
a moment to make up his mind what to do. The strange man
at his door in Grenade on the morning of October 10, 1940,
said, "I was sent here by Henri Duportets [chief of police]. Are
you glad that the Germans are here in France?"

Laporterie stared at him in amazement, trying to size him
up. The man was well dressed, intent, introverted. At this
moment, there was no organized resistance in France, so it
seemed unlikely that this stranger had been sent by de Gaulle
or the British. That he was a German also seemed unlikely to
Laporterie, who now understood something of the German
military mentality. They planned ahead, foreseeing everything,
then used maximum force. They were unlikely to send one spy
in mufti when they could simply order the Vichy police to lead
Gestapo officers on a raid.

Laporterie made up his mind on the spot. "No," he said.

"Do you want to help drive them out?" the stranger asked.

"What do you want?" said Laporterie.

"Take me to Le Penan," said the stranger.

Le Penan, in the free zone on the road to Mont-de-Marsan, was the estate of Pierre Lemée, the mayor of Bretagne-de-Marsan near Bascons. Laporterie knew only that Lemée was up to something. He might be resisting the Germans, or helping them. Rumors were starting that Lemée, his beautiful wife and two daughters were playing games with the Germans, drinking champagne at wild parties. (One especially wild night had already been nicknamed *La nuit des fesses* — Night of the Bottoms.) Was Lemée simply enjoying the occupation? Was he lulling the Germans, with a pretense of cooperation, as Laporterie and some others did, in order to carry out resistance? He decided to take the chance.

He drove the stranger to the private drive approaching Le Penan. The long driveway through oak trees hundreds of years old was barred by two closed gates. Anyone approaching Le Penan would have to get out of his vehicle twice in the half-kilometer driveway to open gates, giving the occupants of the house plenty of time to leave if they needed to. Laporterie stopped the car in front of a small crumbling old château. Mme Lemée greeted him coldly. A haughty woman who believed she was of an aristocratic class destined to rule, she scorned this jumped-up little peasant Laporterie, who made too much of himself with his political ambitions. There was an edge of civility in her greeting only because she had heard he was resisting the Boche on his own. Laporterie, feeling the chill, ignored it.

The stranger, whose real name was Arnould, gave his name as Colonel Olivier. He asked to see her husband. She said he wasn't there. He asked if he could wait. She said that she didn't know how long he would be. Arnould insisted. Finally trusting him, she relented. She called one of her tenant farmers and told him to take Arnould through the oak woods to the *palombier* (pigeon-blind) where Pierre Lemée was in temporary retreat, disgusted with affairs in Vichy France, unable to see how to cope. Arnould thanked her and he and Laporterie walked away through the green-gold light of the open wood. That was how Colonel Arnould, who had landed that morning by parachute, found his way to the hidden *palombier* of Monsieur le Maire de Bretagne-de-Marsan, M. Lemée.

Arnould had been sent by the British to set up one of the first of the Resistance networks, or *réseaux*, in France. His first mission was to locate the vital submarine pens at St-Nazaire so that the Royal Air Force could bomb them.

Arnould was one of dozens of men de Gaulle and Churchill were soon dropping, in competition with each other, all over France. De Gaulle maintained a proud suspicion of "les Anglo-Saxons," which irritated, then finally enraged, Churchill. First of all, Churchill wanted obedience from de Gaulle, which de Gaulle would never grant because he believed that he alone embodied France. Thus rival networks controlled by the English and the Free French spread across France. The French networks, like the governments before them, were split into many factions. Among the communists, some were loyal to Stalin, and therefore respected the Nazi-Soviet pact, and therefore obeyed the Germans or Pétain; some resisted the Germans, anyway. The Vichyites were perhaps the most perplexed of all those French who did not take refuge in immobility. For over a year in France, the conventional wisdom, among people who could understand only what had happened but not what was happening, said that the struggle had ended when France was defeated. The Second World War was over. Obedience to Hitler's New Order had begun. But there were a number of moles in Vichy, who gained strength and numbers as long as Hitler proclaimed victory over Britain without achieving it. One of these moles, a tall brusque commissioner named Jean Pouzelgues, was a friend of Laporterie's.

Pouzelgues came with Barthélémy Duportet, a fellow commissioner, to Grenade looking for someone to cross the demarcation line on a delicate mission. On the terrace of the Hôtel de France in Grenade, near La Petite Maison, one evening Pouzelgues and Duportet outlined the proposition. During the debacle of June 1940, a French regiment had requisitioned the Hôtel de France in Arcachon on the Atlantic coast near Bordeaux for a headquarters and barracks. Retreating south, they had left behind the regimental flag wrapped around some secret documents. The hotel had since been requisitioned by the Wehrmacht for a headquarters-barracks for one of its own units. Pouzelgues asked Laporterie to steal the flag and documents from the barracks, warning him at the same time that another mission sent from Bordeaux had already tried and failed; he was very serious about this mission, which he believed essential to restoring morale in the army. One officer, Captain de Neucheze of the Second Dragoons, probably risked his life by smuggling the Dragoons' regimental flag wrapped around his body under his civilian suit while escaping from Occupied France to Algeria where he planned to rebuild the regiment.

To invade the German barracks on such a mission meant risking jail, possibly deportation. The risk was even greater for Laporterie because once arrested he would almost certainly be denounced for smuggling, forging or transporting illegal aliens. Laporterie asked Pouzelgues when he wanted the job done.

"Within fifteen days," said Pouzelgues.

"Agreed," said Laporterie.

Duportet advised him to speak to the grounds keeper of the hotel, a Frenchman named Bastie, or else to the concierge, Mme Meneteau. He expected, without knowing, that she would be helpful, because her husband was a French army officer imprisoned in Germany. He gave Laporterie a diagram of the building, which Laporterie wrapped around his arm under his shirt sleeve.

That night, without telling Pouzelgues his plan, he slept in Mont-de-Marsan in order to leave early the next day with

André Tachon, who was along because they had previously planned a trip to Bordeaux to collect clothes belonging to Jewish refugees now safe in Vichy France. They were just locking up La Petite Maison in Mont-de-Marsan, ready to leave in the Juvaquatre, when a German patrol car pulled up beside them. The Germans, soldiers in the *Feldgendarmerie*, told Laporterie to turn out the lights in the store because they were shining out into the street, which was against orders.

Annoyed by their officiousness, Laporterie snapped at them, "What are you afraid of? Hitler says you've already won the war."

The policeman decided to teach him a lesson. He pointed out also that the headlights on the Juvaquatre were improperly screened and gave out excessive light. They ordered Laporterie to report to the Kommandantur on two charges the next day.

He drove off angrily past the big air base, which was the real reason the patrol had been so tough with him. Every day huge Focke-Wulf Condors took off from here to range far out over the Atlantic seeking British convoys for the German submarines to attack. Soon the British were asking their spies in France to find the Condor bases, because the planes and submarines were like two hands around the British throat, cutting off the vital convoys from Canada and the Mediterranean.

In Arcachon, Laporterie parked across from the hotel, then walked with Tachon to a café facing the hotel's courtyard. They ordered coffee, as well as Armagnac for Tachon's toothache, as they sat observing the scene. Most of the troops were out on exercises, but there were two German sentinels at the entry. Leaving Tachon to keep watch, Laporterie got up to walk casually across the street to the concierge's lodge. Mme Meneteau was not there.

The man taking her place said she had gone to a different job in Arcachon. Laporterie told the man that he had a message from her husband. The new concierge telephoned the news to her. Overjoyed, she gave him her new address.

As soon as he got there, Laporterie apologized to her for the deception, then told her his mission. She forgave him. Then she wrote a note to the new concierge telling him to admit Laporterie. She also told him exactly where the flag and papers were, wrapped in *La Petite Gironde*, the local newspaper, under a pile of junk abandoned in the attic when the regiment had retreated. Laporterie went back to the hotel, past the sentries, and was admitted to the concierge's lodge. They found the flag in the papers, which Laporterie told the concierge to destroy, all under the eyes of the German soldiers who could see him through the window of the concierge's lodge. Laporterie calmly took an aperitif with the concierge, then strolled out with the flag in a kit bag, offering a cigarette to the Germans. "*Nicht,*" they refused in surprise.

They drove to the port to buy several dozen oysters, which they dumped in a bucket Laporterie had brought for the purpose. The bucket went on top of the bag containing the flag. Tachon drove home with Laporterie sitting beside him, his legs spread around the big bucket. At the border in Mont-de-Marsan, Laporterie offered the guards a dozen oysters, which they accepted.

By chance that afternoon, Duportet and some other officers from Pau, which had become the new district capital for the Bascons region after the demarcation line put Mont-de-Marsan in the occupied zone, came to Bascons to discuss food problems with the mayor. Laporterie invited them for a drink at his mother-in-law's house. The salon of this house, like his own, was hung thick with clothes he had brought over for the refugees.

"Don't forget the flag now, Laporterie," Duportet said.

"You gave me fifteen days. I've still got fourteen to give it a try," Laporterie replied jauntily. Then he added, "However, maybe I have something that will interest you."

While Duportet stared in amazement, Laporterie rolled out the flag.

Duportet embaced him joyfully, and they gazed at it with tears in their eyes, pride in France returning to them.

The flag belonged to the Fifty-second Machine Gun Regiment of Indo-China (the French colony that included Viet Nam).

CHAPTER 5

Spreading the Net

THE WAR BLEW away the worst of aristocratic selfishness, bringing in a new wave of cooperative democratic feeling. The rich, cultivated Poidlouë family of the Château de Myredé, directly across the highway from Le Penan, showed Laporterie no cold condescension, but a trust that changed to friendship under the force of oppression.

Charles Poidlouë, who owned a prosperous optical-supply company in Paris, had neglected his business in order to fly new airplanes as a test pilot for the French air force. He also wrote dramas for stage and film. He and his Spanish wife, Julienne, owned an apartment on the rue Pallu in a fashionable district of Paris. Many people of his social class were indifferent during the war, a minority collaborated with the Germans, and a greater minority joined the Resistance, as he did. Both he and Julienne helped refugees, airmen and prisoners of war from the first hour. Hunted by the Gestapo in Paris for hiding refugees, Poidlouë and Julienne fled south with a refugee friend to Mont-de-Marsan on February 12, 1941.

Poidlouë hoped to cross the line at Mont-de-Marsan to his château, but he saw right away that there were too many Germans patrolling the line. The Germans had decided to crack down on Mont-de-Marsan, where it seemed to them that there was an abnormally high number of people crossing. The

Poidlouës could not cross there safely. They went along the line eighteen kilometers to St-Sever, where there was less activity, therefore fewer patrols. Here Poidlouë thought they might be able to find a quiet wooded section where they could sneak across at night. They were coming up to the riverbank when Poidlouë heard a German patrol approaching. He told Julienne and their friend to lie down in the bushes while he distracted the patrol. He began to run in the opposite direction. The Germans shouted at him to stop.

He was arrested. They took him to their headquarters in a château with a terrace on the riverbank. As they crossed the terrace, Poidlouë jumped over the parapet. He rolled and staggered more than a hundred meters down the steep bank to the river and swam across it, but was still on the German side. He didn't dare swim up the river to freedom, because the Germans were patrolling a bridge under which he would have had to pass.

He walked by ditches and hedgerows to Mont-de-Marsan. His friend, René Vielle, the mayor of Grenade, was trustworthy, but too far away, on the other side of the line. Poidlouë knew Lemée at Le Penan, but he didn't think Lemée was reliable. Raoul Laporterie, whom he had known casually since the mid-thirties, was regularly passing people, according to Vielle. He might be able to hide in Laporterie's store in Mont-de-Marsan. Poidlouë headed for La Petite Maison.

Meanwhile, Julienne and the refugee had escaped across the line, then walked home to safety. Julienne asked the refugee to go into Grenade and tell René Vielle, who was also the head of a Resistance *réseau*, what had happened. Vielle walked along the main street of Grenade in the dark that night to Laporterie's store. Laporterie was in bed but he came downstairs. He agreed that he would look out for Poidlouë the next morning in Mont-de-Marsan, then went back to bed.

As he went over the line the next morning, Laporterie noticed that the number of soldiers on patrol had increased.

He asked why. The Germans told him that a suspect had escaped from the Gestapo the night before.

Muddy, exhausted, but exhilarated, Poidloué arrived at La Petite Maison about ten in the morning. Laporterie quickly took him through the store up to his office. They decided that Poidloué could not stay in Mont-de-Marsan. Too many Germans were looking for him, with an accurate description of him and his clothing. Laporterie made him discard his *canadienne* sheepskin jacket, giving him a new suit.

"We need a photograph of you for new ID papers," said Laporterie. Poidloué, having foreseen this weeks before, had left the correct size of photograph of himself in a small bag at a house in Mont-de-Marsan belonging to the daughter of one of his tenant farmers at Myredé. Laporterie made a new false ID card for him, together with a genuine *Ausweis*, of which he had his own supply, given him by his old friend Jean Larrieu, the mayor of Mont-de-Marsan. Then he said he would take Poidloué across himself in the Juvaquatre. Poidloué objected, but Laporterie pointed out how dangerous it was for him to stay any longer than absolutely necessary in Occupied France. Poidloué said there was no point in Laporterie's getting arrested because of him. Laporterie said that there would be no danger at all because Poidloué would be crossing with him, the mayor of Bascons, whom the Germans trusted. Finally, the aristocrat gave in to the peasant. They crossed together without incident.

At Myredé, Julienne was overjoyed to see her husband safe. After Poidloué had diverted the Germans his way, Julienne and the refugee had sneaked across the line in darkness, then walked the twenty kilometers, past Le Penan, home to safety. In the salon of her old château, the aristocrat Mme Poidloué embraced the kid from the sticks, Raoul Laporterie, thanking him. This grateful embrace embodied a second French Revolution that was beginning silently in millions of French minds.

In their separate reports, Laporterie and Poidloué gave different versions of this event. Poidloué neglected to mention that he had deliberately drawn the Germans to himself to free his wife and friend, an action that Laporterie did report. Laporterie didn't say that he'd had to argue Poidloué into crossing the line with him because it would be safer for Poidloué, though more dangerous for himself. Only Poidloué did say this.

This sealing of friendships in the name of France happened also for Arnould and Lemée as they infiltrated the forbidden zone in Brittany trying to get photographs and maps of the German submarine pens at St-Nazaire. One of Lemée's contacts was an ex-employee, whom he would now have to ask for help. They also found communist workers in a bar near St-Nazaire who offered to help. The communists were supposed to help Hitler who was Russia's ally at the time, but they paid no attention to Stalin now, or to ancient grudges against rich landowners like Lemée. They readily agreed to sneak Arnould's tiny lapel camera into the base. The photographs, which were then smuggled over the line at Mont-de-Marsan, guided the RAF bombers to the pens. Lemée, Arnould and the communists, like most Frenchmen from now on, put the liberation of France, which meant their own freedom, ahead of all other aims.

A Resistance *réseau* (network) comprised several small cells. Within each cell every member was intensely loyal to the others, but little liaison existed among the *réseaux*, mainly because it was safer to limit knowledge in case a captured person was tortured. Some of the *réseaux* sprang up spontaneously, like Laporterie's, some were planted deliberately by agents flown in by Churchill or de Gaulle, each of whom, mistrusting the other, preferred to have his own agents inside France. Among all three kinds of *réseau* were many political variations, some communist, some socialist, some democratic capitalist. Others, peripheral to the main Resistance movement that fought violence with violence, were non-violent groups based on the Christian ethic, whose main aim was to save lives.

All along the demarcation line, as on the frontiers with Spain and Switzerland, men and women risked their freedom for others in touble. The penalties imposed by the Germans, not severe at first, grew much harsher as they realized the extent of the illegal traffic. Within six months, the price a person had to pay to be passed rose from about 150 francs to at least 5000. Letters were by then worth five to ten francs each. Laporterie and Tachon charged nothing.

They passed not only whole families but also their clothing, jewelry, paintings, furs and gold. Laporterie played his part with a reckless bravado that sometimes made his friends crack up with laughter. Tachon once caught Laporterie in the middle of the main square in Grenade showing an admiring crowd the oil can that Tachon had made with a false bottom to carry papers and letters. Tachon also had to warn him that it was stupid to lift the hood of the Juvaquatre to pull out documents every time he returned to Grenade at night, because there were informers in the town. The mayor himself was straddling the fence between the Germans and the Resistance.

After the Germans started tightening the inspections and regulations, arresting *passeurs*, more people than ever came to Laporterie for help. From Lille, Cambrai, Cannes, Lyon, Marseille, Pau, Bordeaux, Paris, on letterhead, by telegram, on scraps of paper, nearly always with deepest gratitude, thanks in advance of service, excuses for troubling him, but in the interest of a sick son, a weak daughter, a missing father . . . in the elegant handwriting of the era, with a flourish to the capital M like the curl of a dandy's mustache, or in capital letters pasted on gray-green telegram paper, or on the limp gray cardboard of the postcards supplied by the Germans with preprinted messages containing a few blanks, all these usually containing a cautious code, to be answered in code, as if these naive locutions could stop the determined Germans better than the French army had. These letters and telegrams went on through 1940, 1941, 1942, all with the same object, to save from *les féroces* — the Boche — a son, or a daughter, a lover, friend, mother, father, all the beloved people called in code "the package."

A letter from an anxious mother in Spain asking about her son, addressed simply to Laporter, France, arrived safely at La Petite Maison. People used to crowd around the store in Grenade every morning waiting to see him with their requests. When he and Tachon arrived in Mont-de-Marsan, there would be a crowd waiting there, as well. Tachon was horrified once to find a man walking among German soldiers through the square in Mont-de-Marsan reading a letter that described how easy it was to cross with Laporterie. He could not make Laporterie more cautious, even though the penalty now for carrying just a couple of letters over the line was to be thrown in Fort-du-Ha jail near Bordeaux, where all the inmates were in effect held as hostages for any crimes committed by the French against German soldiers. The penalty the hostages paid was to be shot or deported to a concentration camp in Germany, probably to die.

On one single trip that winter, Laporterie carried 1500 letters over the line. His record was more than fifty people passed in one day from Occupied France to Vichy France. While he and Tachon carried on so recklessly, other *passeurs* grew so cautious that they checked out their potential passengers almost as carefully as the police did.

One *passeur*, who lived north of Bordeaux, spent a whole day checking out a stranger seeking passage, only to discover that the stranger was exactly as he said — the head of a Resistance network farther north, the man who became famous later as Colonel Rémy. The courage of another brave agent nearly failed him one night before a planned crossing because he kept imagining the dogs finding him in the woods, the searchlights picking him out for the machine guns. Some did the crossing concealed under sacks of coal, or in hay, or disguised as nuns. One clung to the underside of a locomotive while his friend in the cab drove slowly and stopped just inside the Vichy line to let him escape. The Rabbi Netter, after his crossing near the river Cher, wrote in his journal: "Ah, what relief, what joy, what happiness to escape such danger, such a death. From my most profound being, I give thanks to Providence for leading me out safe and sound from this extreme danger."[1]

Nissim Yaeche was also worried about the risks Laporterie ran. Once, as they were sitting in Laporterie's upstairs kitchen over the store in Grenade after the 9:20 BBC news, Yaeche asked him why he ran such great risks to bring letters over the line for other people, risks that were growing worse almost every week as the jail terms grew longer. Laporterie replied, "Just think, among those letters there are probably a lot from mothers who haven't had any news of their children for a long time. It really warms my heart to bring them good news."

Yaeche was so touched by that reply that he remembered it for the rest of his life. He never needed to ask again why Laporterie did anything.

Laporterie had an insouciant attitude toward the Germans, which amounted almost to contempt. This was perfectly in character for him. He'd always had an ambivalent attitude toward authority, for which Germans in general had only respect. He wore easily the uniform of authority — the suit, shoes, tie, hat, accent — he was always well organized, he disliked communists, he believed in the myth of the French army, he normally abided by the rules of the state to such an extent that although he opposed Pétain in everything he did during the Resistance, he ended up defending the paternalistic old marshal after the war. This was the kid emerging ambitious from the sticks, seeing that the road to get ahead lay between the lines of established authority. Opposition would get him nowhere because he was alone; cooperation, at which he was a master, would enable him to rise in the public service. On the other hand, the Laporterie who was smarter and better organized than most of the people he met, who was educating himself by his own efforts, refused to be hampered by stupid rules. He could be cooperative to the point of servility, or recklessly independent.

Working close to the Germans was the best way, Laporterie thought, but this meant confronting them alone, like the bull-wrestling toreador in the finale of the Portuguese corrida, which he had often seen in the bullring at Mont-de-Marsan. The bull is lured to one side of the circular ring. From the other side of the circle, the toreador advances directly at the bull with his back arched and his steps prancing, but with no weapon or cape, shouting, "*Taureau, hé, taureau!*" Behind him in a straight line away from the bull are eight other men. The bull charges. Still facing the bull, the toreador runs backward into the others, now also running slowly backward. When the bull is close, the toreador leaps over the bull's lowered head, grabbing the bull's throat. The other men instantly swarm around, grabbing neck, ears, horns, stilling the bull with their weight. Once he is stilled, one of the men grabs him by the tail, the others let go, and the bull circles tightly around trying to gore the man attached to his tail, whom he can just see but not reach. Laporterie facing the Germans was like the toreador, taking the first shock, but he was invariably supported by the friends lined up behind him.

Abel Oppenheimer, Bezos's friend and parliamentary secretary from Paris, came to Mont-de-Marsan soon after the armistice to work in Laporterie's store under his protection. The conservative Oppenheimer shared many of Laporterie's traits. He was a lanky, good-looking man, always well dressed in a suit. He was both dignified and humorous, like Laporterie. He enjoyed his life, even during these scary times in Mont-de-Marsan. He liked especially to go drinking and talking with Laporterie in the cafés. Laporterie drank a lot in those days; Oppenheimer had always drunk too much. Laporterie would down glasses of Noilly vermouth while Oppenheimer drank the much stronger Armagnac. Soon the two of them were using the intimate *tu* like boyhood friends. Oppenheimer addressed

Laporterie by his first name, and Laporterie affectionately called Oppenheimer "Friquet," his nickname. Raoul was delighted to find in the well-educated Friquet the wide knowledge he craved. Friquet found Raoul a stimulating companion. From the first day, they talked animatedly about history, literature, the war, France, politics.

They sat in the Café de la Poste, whose owners knew what they were doing. Here they held court in the open, receiving strangers who had come to Mont-de-Marsan on the chance of getting over the line somehow. Others came to the little city knowing about Laporterie by name only. They would ask around for who might help them, or where Laporterie could be found. Then, in Laporterie's office, Friquet and Raoul would arrange the papers and the times. Occasionally, to save time, Oppenheimer would telephone a description of the passenger to Laporterie's Bascons secretary, Dumartin, who would then get busy preparing the papers. Because the telephone lines that crossed the demarcation line were sometimes tapped by the Germans, Oppenheimer usually made these calls from one of the public phones in the post office, where he judged what to say into the phone by the expression on the face of Renée Darriet, a friend of Laporterie's who worked in the post office. She always knew when the Germans were listening.

Laporterie gave Oppenheimer a job in La Petite Maison keeping the books. It amused Laporterie to call this distinguished man, a parliamentary secretary, whose sister was a countess, "my private secretary." Oppenheimer would also help Laporterie write reports on what was going on in France for the British, who needed accurate up-to-date information for their spies. Changes occurred so quickly in France that even an escaped native of the region parachuted back in a few months later could betray himself to an observant German or Vichy policeman by not knowing some important new regulation.

Oppenheimer and Laporterie were driving a rented car back from Bordeaux one bright day in early June 1941, singing as they drove through the cool pine woods of Landes. "*Ah, la vie est belle*," said Oppenheimer. They had eaten and drunk well, they were going back to friends in Mont-de-Marsan with lots of mail, Oppenheimer would see his wife, Blanche, that night — everything on the warm June afternoon seemed pretty good despite the war. They were stopped by the *Feldgendarmerie* at the control post at Captieux, where Oppenheimer, giddy with booze, fumbled open his wallet looking for his identity papers. Out onto the road fell several letters he was going to pass over the line for friends, as well as some documents that revealed he had friends in the Resistance. Oppenheimer stared dizzily at the envelopes as he reached down for them, but the German was faster. He picked them up, studying the postmarks and addresses.

"Where did you get these?"

"I don't know," Oppenheimer said.

"You don't know? How can you not know?"

"I mean, a friend of mine in Bordeaux asked me to mail these in Grenade because it's outside the occupied zone. Then they can go to Toulouse."

"Get out," said the soldier. "You're under arrest." He ordered Laporterie out of the car, too, searched him and then impounded the car, leaving Laporterie to find his own way home, while the Germans did a thorough search. Laporterie went home by taxi, not singing.

The next day he discovered that Oppenheimer was being held in Fort-du-Ha jail in Bordeaux. Laporterie took him food and new clothes, and reassured him that he was also taking care of Blanche. Because Jews in the occupied zone were not required to mark Jew on their ID papers until after September 26, 1940, when Oppenheimer and Blanche were already safe with unmarked papers and working for Laporterie, they were not discovered, nor did anyone denounce them for failing to register as Jews. With the help of his friend Camille Lacoste and probably a bribe Laporterie finally managed to have Oppenheimer released on December 4. Oppenheimer was not chastened. He and Laporterie carried on almost exactly as before.

Soon after this, Laporterie discovered that the Germans in Mont-de-Marsan were looking for someone to help them censor mail and to do some translating back and forth between French and German. He said that he knew a German-speaking Frenchman who would be glad to help them censor mail going across the line, or to fill in as a translator when needed. So Oppenheimer, like Laporterie, threw his arms around the German bull. He worked for the rest of the war in the store, and at the same time was a translator and censor for the Germans in Mont-de-Marsan. As a result he was sometimes in a position to pass on sensitive information about the air base to his friends in the Resistance.

Even though Oppenheimer had done time in the dismal Fort-du-Ha, his offense was relatively common, and the Germans, well organized as they were, did not always check as thoroughly as they might people they hired for relatively minor jobs such as translator. They had only about 10,000 men in France doing the kind of secret police work necessary to capture resisters like Oppenheimer and Laporterie.[2] According to their own calculations they were understaffed, certainly at first, by at least two-thirds.[3] The war in the west seemed to them won. The French had caved in, there was little resistance, so they ran the country with minimal force. Once the war became global, they were short of manpower even at the front, so the rear echelons suffered. All this meant that they depended heavily on the French themselves to help police France in the interests of Germany. Among the French police, of course, were many men who secretly sympathized with the Laporteries and Tachons. By this time, Laporterie and his friends in Mont-de-Marsan had in fact penetrated the Wehrmacht and Gestapo office organizations so well that they could sometimes protect their friends in the Resistance. Often when the Gestapo came to arrest someone, they found he had just left for another place.

When the Germans arrived in the other place, he had not yet arrived, and so on.

The Germans had taken over the racetrack in Mont-de-Marsan, which was adjacent to the air base, and were busy building new runways to add to the existing ones. Friends of Laporterie's who worked at the air base discovered that the longer runways were designed to accommodate a new long-range version of the Focke-Wulf Condor, carrying at least three tons of bombs, which Hitler and Goering were already using to drop on convoys heading across the Atlantic from Canada to England. The new long-range Condors were to be used to bomb North America. Already the range of the Condor was approaching the distance necessary to hit the big Canadian naval base in Halifax, where the convoys assembled before heading east. The engineers and pilots at Mont-de-Marsan were now experimenting with various devices to add to the range, including the longer runway to give the heavily loaded planes the added speed necessary to take off. They were also developing extra fuel tanks that could be attached to the wings and, once emptied, could be jettisoned in flight. To the Resistance spies on the ground, the new runways did not seem particularly newsworthy, but the word was passed on to Britain regardless.

All this work, which employed hundreds of French civilians at the base, was a change in the war almost as significant as the fall of France. Hitler had written in *Mein Kampf* fifteen years before that: "If land was desired in Europe, it could be obtained by and large only at the expense of Russia, and this meant that the new Reich must again set itself on the march along the road of the Teutonic Knights of old, to obtain by the German sword sod for the German plow and daily bread for the nation. For such a policy there was but one ally in Europe: England."[4] But instead of an ally, Hitler had a recalcitrant Churchill.

Unable to invade Britain to conquer her by land, he had hoped to beat her in the air. After that failed, he settled on submarine warfare to starve her. With England neutralized, Hitler could at last implement his great scheme to extend German rule over all of Eastern Europe. When he attacked his Russian allies and the Japanese fell on the Americans in 1941, the Second World War was over. The war that began among Germany, Britain, Russia, Japan, the United States and China, which was ended only with an overwhelming nuclear attack, was World War III.

The *réseau* of Charles Poidlouë, under its chief, M. Franz Van Den Brouck d'Obrenan, boulevard Richard-Wallace, Neuilly, was centered in Paris. Help was needed, Poidlouë told Laporterie, to send refugees, agents and downed flyers south to the free zone, and thence on out to Spain, where Julienne had connections. Would Laporterie offer the use of his network? Laporterie agreed. So bit by bit, by word of mouth to trusted friends, the Resistance grew. Two little local *réseaux*, such as Laporterie's and Poidlouë's, suddenly expanded in one night to a unit that straddled France. In fact, Poidlouë was a member of two other *réseaux*, one named Sauterelles, the other Les Petites Ailes. Laporterie made new papers for Charles and Julienne, then drove them back across the line.

The Poidlouës reached Paris safely, where they began sending south a new stream of refugees. Along with some Allied flyers who had been shot down came people from the fashionable world of Paris. Jacques Pills, the husband of the famous singer Edith Piaf, came to Laporterie for identity papers and passage, which Laporterie gave him. Clara Malraux, the wife of writer André Malraux, took a card from Laporterie in the name of Marie-Claire Lamy. It showed that she was born in the sixteenth district of Paris, which was so typical of the *grand monde* that Proust chose it for the locale for his famous *A la recherche du temps perdu*, the ponderous novel about the sensitive rich of France. The Germans, seeing the card correctly filled out, did not stop to wonder how it was that a woman born in the most snobbish part of Paris had become a shopkeeper in a muddy little four-car village in the sticks.

The thing that counted for the Germans was not that the card described a likely person, but that it was correctly filled out. Mme Malraux passed with her very correct card, ostensibly to join her husband, who was actually one of de Gaulle's top agents, working in the hills of the Dordogne northeast of Grenade.

One of the Rothschilds came to Laporterie for papers and passage, which Laporterie supplied without charge. From the Rothschild estate near Bordeaux later came a case of their best wine, which, Laporterie casually said to the happy Oppenheimer, "will do to quench our thirst." There was a whole convent of nuns, from a convent in the Ardennes, with the abbess. A black woman, who had no counterpart in the birth certificates of Bascons, was passed hiding under a pile of clothes in the back seat of the Juvaquatre.

Laporterie was also passing some refugees in the other direction — into the occupied zone. Two soldiers of the French army were among the crowd one morning outside the store in Grenade, saying they thought it was safe for them to go back to their homes in the north. The Germans had finished rounding up French soldiers to ship back to Germany as slave labor, in defiance of the armistice, so the two young men had left their hideout in Vichy France to try to return to their families. Laporterie saw danger because even if the Germans had officially stopped rounding up soldiers, they would certainly suspect what these two young men were up to. He told them to stop eating for three days, then come back and he would take them across. When they came back, looking tired and gaunt, he gave them new papers with new names and put them into the back of an ambulance he had rented. Tachon, pretending to be an orderly, sat with them. Late at night he had them lie on stretchers, put some bandages on them, then drove to the post, which was closed. He explained to the duty officer that he had two sick people on board who had to go to hospital in Mont-de-Marsan right away. The German checked the papers, as well as the appearance of the patients, then waved them through.

Laporterie sped them to a safe house belonging to a friend of his, where they spent the rest of the night. The next morning, Laporterie got them discharge papers from the hospital. That morning, cured, they were en route home.

CHAPTER **6**

The Worst Winter of the War

MANY PEOPLE in France lived in despairing gloom in the winter of 1940 –41 Huguette Yaeche felt cold all the time in the Laporterie house, except on sunny mornings when she was playing with her young brother, Albert, in the attic. There was almost no fuel for the stove or fireplace. France's fuel, wine, food, cloth, aircraft all disappeared along with the trains carrying them into Germany. For most people in France, the Second World War was already over, thus liberation seemed like a cruel fantasy, torturing people by its hopelessness, rather than inspiring them to realize it. For these people, hope only magnified their misery. So Huguette Yaeche, along with the many others in refuge in Bascons, came to depend upon the cheerfulness of Laporterie to lift their spirits. He even managed to bring Mme Yaeche's parents over to Bascons, under false names, to Huguette's delight.

Sarah Yaeche tried once again to persuade her father to stay permanently, but he refused. "I'm not afraid of anything," he said. "I'm not running any risk at all."

Her grandparents left Bascons to go back to Bordeaux while Huguette was up in the attic playing. When she came downstairs she cried because she hadn't said goodbye to them. Her mother tried to calm her by saying they might come again soon. Perhaps she thought that if the Germans did come for her grandparents, Laporterie would still be able to do something at the last minute.

Laporterie's cheerfulness came mainly from his youthful love of life. Even in middle age, as he was then, he liked to boast that he had the reactions of a boy. He was right. His bold driving showed it, as he shimmered among farm trucks in narrow roads around Grenade, or twisted nimbly over curbs around parked trucks in the crowded alleys of Mont-de-Marsan. This ability to react fast in danger was what carried him past the Germans again and again, though it was not true, as some people thought, that he did not plan carefully. According to Georges Dubos, Laporterie and Tachon "industrialized the process" of transporting refugees. Dubos told him he was most imprudent, running terrible risks, but Laporterie was nonchalant. An old Landais saying he liked to quote runs "If you're in danger, look a woman in the eye, a horse in the rear, and a curé from all sides." It was clear that as far as danger was concerned he treated the Germans like priests.

He enjoyed what he was doing so much that he agreed to teach one of the Alsatian refugees in Bascons, Jules Pêcheur, how to pass people through German controls. Pêcheur had heard he was about to be returned to his native province, which Hitler had incorporated into Germany. Laporterie showed him the tricks of the passeur, which Pêcheur then used to save refugees in Alsace. Perhaps the most inspiring lesson for Pêcheur came from the indefatigable courage of Laporterie. As the villagers and his family said, "He is a man who will never accept defeat." Pêcheur was himself denounced in Alsace for his work, fled from the Germans and came once again to Bascons, where Laporterie gave him new papers and a place to stay.

As he took risks for himself, Laporterie inflicted them on others, including his family and everyone in Bascons. That included young Albert Yaeche, who at the age of twelve was supposed to be going to school. Laporterie, with Nissim's approval, gave young Albert missions to run for the Resistance. He was nicknamed Agent Popote (Little Pot) as he took papers and messages across the line for Laporterie and others. He was so busy that he was sometimes away from school for days.

Agent Popote, along with many others working unknowingly beside him, attracted the attention of the very able Friedrich Dohse, commander of the regional Gestapo headquarters in Bordeaux. Dohse suspected that maps, photographs and general information about the submarine pens all along the Atlantic coast had been illegally made by the French Resistance, then smuggled out to England. At this point in the war, the submarine attacks on the great convoys that steamed over from Halifax, Sydney, Saint John and Montreal to England were crippling the British-Canadian war effort. The RAF was searching for the exact sites of the sub pens and the Focke-Wulf Condor bases, which were highly vulnerable to bombers. Mont-de-Marsan, both a transfer point for agents with information and, because of its air base, a potential target for the RAF, became a high priority for Dohse.

In March 1941, shortly after Poidloue's escape — and successful return to Paris via Mont-de-Marsan — three Gestapo men in suits parked their black Citroën front-wheel-drive sedan in the muddy street in front of the *mairie* in Bascons. From his window across the street, Joseph Farbos watched them park and go into the building. Although he was afraid of them, Farbos was too excited to stay inside, so he joined the other villagers who were standing watching.

The Gestapo, having missed Laporterie, came back downstairs disappointed. One of them seized Farbos, rammed a pistol up against his nose and demanded to know where Laporterie was. Farbos said he didn't know. Suddenly the Gestapo man took away the pistol, then offered Farbos a cigarette.

"No, thanks, I don't smoke, but thank you very much," said Farbos, who was quite afraid. The Gestapo got into the car and drove away.

They had searched the files, Dumartin later told Laporterie when he came to inspect the *mairie*. There was nothing out of line, as far as the Gestapo could see. The careful preparations were barely enough. There was nothing for the Gestapo to find except the real birth certificates, which were written, as they all are in French villages, chronologically in a bound book, year following year, so that no falsification is possible, unless the forger is willing to patiently inscribe hundreds of pages in French copperplate in a new book, duplicating the real certificates while inserting the false. As the Gestapo left Bascons, they drove past the graveyard where all the names that Laporterie had used were staring them in the eye. The same month that the Gestapo searched Laporterie's office at Bascons, they caught a young man named Jean Piot crossing the line illegally. Piot was shot.[1]

Yaeche, seeing that the Gestapo could easily cross the line to search for even such a trusted official as Laporterie, well inside the free zone, almost certainly decided that day to leave Bascons. What if Laporterie and Tachon had not been quite so well prepared? Surely the Gestapo would have forced them, with threats or torture, to disclose the names of the refugees, as well as the agents, perhaps including Agent Popote.

Laporterie's lawbreaking, which had saved Yaeche's family, was now endangering them. The Germans themselves were breaking the terms of the armistice every day with their thefts, their racist attacks on French citizens, their refusal to send back the one and a half million prisoners as agreed under the terms of the armistice. The demarcation line, so difficult for the refugees to cross, was no safeguard now.

Yaeche decided the family should go to the *département* of Lot-et-Garonne, where they would try to get visas to emigrate to North Africa or to the United States. He said goodbye with tears in his eyes to Laporterie and to Laure. As he wrote later from Marseille, he had been so distressed at leaving all his good friends that he could not speak. "I got used to seeing you often, and little by little, affection entered in. I got into the habit of coming to see you almost every day to say hello, to talk with you or your wife or her mother, and because they always welcomed me so warmly I felt I was in my own home."

Yaeche's dream of emigrating soon evaporated. With Sarah and the children he moved into the house of Sarah's sister and brother-in-law, Elie Safaty, in Limoges. As always, Yaeche kept his faith in the goodness of others by noticing every small sign of it. He told Laporterie that the people of Limoges were "very good Frenchmen," like the people of Bascons. But Limoges proved impossible for the family. Relations with the Safatys were strained by that family's poverty, as well as by constant fear, like a low-grade virus that never is cured. Soon the prefecture ordered all the unemployed, like Yaeche, to leave town, and so help alleviate the housing shortage. Where could they go?

Amid mutual protestations of goodwill, good wishes for each other's health, advice on caring for one's health, inquiries about each other's health, Laporterie and Yaeche wrote back and forth making arrangements. Laporterie found a place called Lestelle-Betharram, a village high in the Pyrénées near Pau. Because the Germans had ordered all Jews to sew a bright yellow cloth Star of David on their clothes, announcing at the same time that "everyone who helps the Jews will share their fate," Yaeche decided now that he had to hide from the Germans everything about his family. Laporterie gave them certificates of Catholic baptism in the name of Grenier, dated at Bascons. So at the very moment Yaeche was no longer a Jew in the eyes of the Germans, Laporterie became one.

In Lestelle-Betharram the newly baptized Yaeches pretended to be Catholic by going every Sunday to Mass. Young Roger, only six years old, was ordered on pain of death never to say again the name Yaeche, never to think of himself as a Yaeche, but to become, even in dreams, Grenier.

For the same reason Yaeche had to decide whether to run to Marseille, Laporterie had to decide whether to continue his trade in refugees. Obviously the Germans were growing suspicious, which increased the danger to him, as well as the possibility that any help he now offered to the refugees might be the bait for a trap. But finally he decided to continue without any change, because the Gestapo, having suspected him and found nothing, were now so sure of him that they hadn't even bothered to pick him up for questioning in Mont-de-Marsan. He was bullet-proof for a little while anyway, or so he wanted to believe. It would be hard to leave the fascination and excitement of Mont-de-Marsan. If anything did develop in the future, he now had a network of informants and friends in the town who would warn him. His old friend Mayor Larrieu, playing a very dangerous double game, cooperated with the Germans in minor ways, while helping Laporterie by giving him news, advice and blank *Ausweise*. There was an Austrian at the air base who hated the Nazis because of the Anschluss, Hitler's annexation of Austria, there was a helpful Alsatian named Herz at the checkpoint, there was his friend Renée Darriet, an agent of the Marco Polo *réseau* who worked in the post office, listening to the phone, reading the telegrams, there was Friquet translating for the Germans, and there was his dear friend Mme Pointis and her daughter, whom he loved, and who doted on him. There was also Georgette Dumoulin, taxi driver, whom he had known since the days when they both hustled goods from the backs of their wagons in the countryside.

It was this network of friends and moles that probably saved Laporterie's life, because now the Germans were more reliant than ever on French police to help them track resisters and *passeurs*.[2]

Laporterie and Tachon assisted by Dumoulin went on shuttling back and forth between Bordeaux and Mont-de-Marsan, bringing carfuls of suitcases, clothing, textiles, fur coats, gold, diamonds, paintings, maps, mail, messages — whatever his passengers or the Resistance needed. The profits from La Petite Maison were shrinking because of shortages caused by the Germans, but he continued to help refugees free of charge. He paid for the stamps on the documents and letters, or for the hotel bills in Grenade if he had been unable to find a spare room in the big hostel that Bascons was becoming.

He did not ask for money because it would have undone half the good he was trying to do. Most of the people he brought over needed every sou they had to stay alive. What good would it have done to bring them to a safe place to starve? Still, some of the refugees were so grateful that they pressed gifts on him. The Rothschilds had given him a case of their best wine; the Yaeches, with typical grace, gave him a painting by a student of Corot's, M. Angel; a Bordeaux furrier, who had been so terrified of crossing that he postponed it for weeks, was so grateful for his safe arrival in Grenade that he presented a beautiful Persian lamb coat to Madame Laporterie, a gift that was doubly welcome in the cold of that winter.

Laporterie paid also for the Juvaquatre's fuel, which was expensive and hard to find. His good friend Dupeyron of Mont-de-Marsan, a garage owner whose wife was a famous long-distance flyer and also a good friend of Laporterie's, stole gasoline for Laporterie from the air base where he worked part-time. It was high-octane aviation fuel, designed to power Condors across the Atlantic, not the engine in the little Juvaquatre, which it caused to turn red-hot. Laporterie had to replace the spark leads many times because the motor over-heated so badly, but the block held. He also wangled a foul-smelling fuel made of pine trees, which, thanks to Napoleon III, had been planted all over Landes to replace the forests cut down previously by the wastrel king, Louis XIV.

Laporterie continued to deal smoothly with the Germans, even making suits for the commanding officers. He used that connection, along with a little bribery, to help his friends get out of trouble. For the bribery, he and friends raised pigs in Bascons, had them butchered and took bribes of fresh pork down to the jail to ransom his Jews. There was an anti-German joke he delighted in:

> Yvonne and Yvan meet in the street in Paris one day and Yvonne says, "Did you hear what happened in the street outside my apartment last night?"
>
> "No," says Yvan.
>
> "Well," says Yvonne, "a Jew killed a Nazi at about nine-thirty and ate his heart right in the street."
>
> "I know you're fooling," says Yvan. "First, a Nazi has no heart. Second, Jews don't eat pork. And third, at nine-thirty everyone is listening to the BBC."

Sometimes if Laporterie was out of meat or bolts of cloth, he used money, but he was never charged with offering a bribe. The Germans probably felt they were indulging this friendly little guy who obviously had no interest in politics. Just as Hitler spurned all Premier Laval's offers to help Germany win the war in return for letting France share the spoils, the field officers felt an amused contempt for the conquered French. After all, the heroic Pétain had been forced to his knees, so why not a tailor in the backwoods of Landes?

Laporterie and Tachon kept on as if nothing had happened. Laporterie carried hundreds of letters over the line in a single pass, at a time when crossing even one letter would get the *passeur* months in jail, but he paid no attention to the warnings of his friends, such as Georges Dubos, who were stupefied at the risks he took. André Tachon at least used to search his passengers for anything incriminating before attempting to cross them, but Raoul Laporterie rarely did.

He consented to cross a Jewish woman dentist from Arcachon in August 1941. She wanted to cross with her two daughters to go and live in the free zone with her son, a dentist crossed earlier by Laporterie. Laporterie told her that she was to carry "nothing dangerous in your bag, no traces of your name, no money, nothing." The woman agreed, but when they stopped at the barrier Laporterie knew right away something was wrong because they were all ordered out of the car for a search. This was unprecedented, but Laporterie remained outwardly calm as the dentist was taken into the cabin to be searched.

Several Austrians had replaced the Germans on the line, and one came out with the news that they had discovered gold bars on the dentist, who was now under arrest with her daughters. They searched the Juvaquatre thoroughly, finding nothing, then patted down Laporterie and let him go on to Grenade.

That night he and Tachon talked it over. Should they continue their work back in Mont-de-Marsan? They had been let go once, and it seemed there was now no danger. But if the Gestapo searched La Petite Maison in Mont-de-Marsan, they would find all kinds of seals, French flags and incriminating letters, which would precipitate a more intensive search, probably incriminating others, as well.

They drove back the next morning. At the store Mme Hortense, Laporterie's loyal friend and assistant manager, was very upset because five men in suits and carrying briefcases had come to the store earlier asking for him. She was sure they were Gestapo, so she'd said to them naively, "He's not here right now. Come back around noon — he's usually in by then."

A few minutes later, in came a uniformed French policeman, the Alsatian named Herz who had befriended Laporterie. As soon as they were alone he said, "Your wife has been arrested." Laporterie thought quickly, then remembered that he had passed the dentist with Laure's *Ausweis*. "Yes, but she's not my wife," he said. He explained briefly.

Herz said, "You know, you're in big trouble. I just came from the *Kommandantur* and I told them that I wanted to see you. You'd better get the hell out of here and not come back."

Laporterie thanked him, but instead of leaving he took some files, seals and papers, then walked quickly along one side of the Place de la Poste to his new store, Erely, which was being renovated. He was packing the Bascons seals, the illegal blank *Ausweise* given him by Mayor Larrieu and other dangerous things into sacks of coal when André Tachon entered the store as calmly as he could.

"They're there," he said. "We have to go. Right now."

Laporterie dropped several hundred unopened letters into a half-plastered wall, then to the amazement of the plasterer said, "Finish it and shut your mouth." Then they ran out to the car with the sacks of coal, racks of suits, cloth and dresses. In the loaded Juvaquatre, with its clouds of stinking fumes and red-hot block, they bucked out of Mont-de-Marsan heading for . . . where?

They couldn't cross at their normal checkpoint on the road to Grenade, which was the only legal place permitted on their own permanent *Ausweise.* "We'd be walking into the wolf's mouth," said Laporterie. They started toward St-Sever along the highway that bordered the line. They saw many uniformed Germans with leashed guard dogs patroling the area where all the trees had been chopped down for better visibility along the line.

"It's not worth it," Laporterie said. "Too dangerous around here. Let's go back to Villeneuve."

At Villeneuve, a village on the other side of Mont-de-Marsan, they came to a checkpoint, which they had used once or twice before, where the guards recognized them. A German officer with magnificent red stripes down his trousers came out to the car and said, "But Monsieur le Chef de La Petite Maison, this isn't the road to Grenade, where you're supposed to cross."

Laporterie said, "Listen, if you let me pass so I can drop off all these clothes, then tomorrow I'll come back with some cloth for my store."

The officer said, "Could you make me a suit?"

Laporterie thought, Heaven is descending on my head. Thank you, little Jesus. To the officer he said, "Yes, I can."

"When should I come in to the store?" the officer asked.

"Tomorrow," Laporterie replied. The barrier was lifted. They crossed into the free zone.

CHAPTER 7

A Dangerous Comedy

OFTEN AFTER they had fooled the Germans, Tachon and Laporterie would laugh, savoring the details of their escapade like boys. This time was too close for laughter. They were both grim even when they were deep inside the free zone. They both knew they might not be safe even there, because many of the Vichy police cooperated closely with the Germans.

Tachon headed for Aire-sur-l'Adour where he had friends. Laporterie did not even go home until three nights had passed. First he telephoned the uncle of the dentist's daughters in Mont-de-Marsan to find out what had happened. The dentist had been arrested for smuggling and was sure to receive a long sentence, but the children had been released to the custody of their uncle. Then, before going to stay with friends outside Grenade, Raoul telephoned Laure to tell her he was safe.

Laporterie believes in Nietzsche's maxim "The troubles that do not kill you improve you," but it was not easy to see any improvement as he took up the life of the fugitive himself. He rejoined Laure and Irène for a few days, then set out to see friends in Pau who he was sure would help him to reestablish himself in Resistance work in Vichy France. There were still lots of refugees who needed help getting new papers, baptismal certificates, finding jobs or housing.

In September 1941, Laporterie received an odd request from a diamond merchant in Marseille who was in trouble with a *passeur*. The merchant, Brachfeld, had entrusted to the *passeur* a box full of diamonds just before crossing the line. Brachfeld told Laporterie that the diamonds had been hidden in the *gazogène* — a small machine that burns solid fuel — of a car to get across the line. The diamonds, according to the story the *passeur* told Brachfeld, had been burned in the *gazogène*. Brachfeld knew, of course, that diamonds can't burn at such low temperatures, so he knew he was being robbed. He had no other means of support. He was in a very difficult position, lacking money, local friends. A court case would expose him to the danger of denunciation, which would lead to certain death in a concentration camp. What could he do? At first things looked bleak, as his nephew Max Perlberger wrote to Laporterie from Marseille on September 9:

Dear friend,
    You can imagine what kind of shape we were in getting back to the family. The despair of my uncle, his wife and the children was indescribable. Now the only ray of hope left to us is you. My uncle asks me to thank you. But how can I thank you enough? Only God can pay you for all the good you have done for everyone.
    I hope that soon you will give us news and that you will do the impossible to help us out of this hole we so stupidly fell into.

Laporterie replied, asking for more details and for a power of attorney so that he could deal with the case on his own, protecting Brachfeld. Brachfeld then wrote back to him a week later:

I have complete confidence in you, dear M. Laporterie, and I ask you once more to do the impossible for us and save the lives of a lot of people (15). I am convinced that he himself regrets what he has done, but doesn't know how to undo his fault and become honest again. I think we should wait a little longer before taking him to court, because one can always do that. First it is best to try all other available means, even if there aren't many.

I thank you very much, dear M. Laporterie, and I will never forget that there still exist noble men like you who are always ready to help unfortunate people.

Laporterie considered going to the *passeur* in question, but he did not trust the man, because he thought he might be playing a double game to his own advantage, deceiving both the Germans and the French. Of course, Laporterie himself was selling uniforms to the Germans, giving them presents and at the same time defying their laws. But he was calm in his conscience, while he could not be sure of Brachfeld's *passeur*'s motives. If the man was stealing from Brachfeld, Laporterie risked being denounced for taking up the defense of Brachfeld. Finally he decided to take the chance. He had the great pleasure of recovering the diamonds right away, to present intact to Brachfeld within a week.[1]

By this time, Sarah Yaeche had heard that because of new racist legislation, her parents had been deprived of their furniture by the police in Bordeaux. Before the couple could make up their minds what to do next, they were arrested. Laporterie inquired, but there was never again any news of them. What happened to Sarah's parents can only be surmised from evidence given at the Nuremberg trials.

The Nazis were trying to round up 50,000 stateless Jews in Vichy France "for shipment to the east." One of the trains that had been sent to Bordeaux for them waited with only 150 refugees aboard. Premier Laval was asked to find some French Jews to make up a load. He refused. "The train, due to leave on July 15, 1942, had to be canceled," said Theodor Danneker,

Adolf Eichmann's representative in Paris. Eichmann was furious because he imagined that his prestige was at stake. He'd had to conduct lengthy negotiations about the trains with the *Reichsminister* of transportation, and now Danneker had canceled it. He was ashamed to report this to the SS. Momentarily discouraged, he almost decided not to bother with Jews from France again because France was not a reliable source of internees for the camps.

Laval and the French police had on several occasions said they wanted to see the children of Jews go with their parents to the Reich. Danneker pressed their case. On July 20, Eichmann telephoned him from Berlin to say that Jewish children and old people could be deported, not only people capable of work. Probably because of this, Sarah's parents were taken from their bare apartment to another train, this one filled with all kinds of Jews — young, old, stateless, French — who were taken to Drancy, the big transfer camp. It was here that the trains were assembled to go to the final destination.[2]

Huguette Yaeche could not stop her tears, because she had not come down from the attic to say goodbye on that last day in Bascons.

All this was the result of decisions by Hitler, communicated to Heinrich Himmler, head of the SS, in the summer of 1941. Hitler told Himmler that he had already decided upon "the final solution" of the Jewish problem. This policy was promulgated to a formal meeting of undersecretaries of various ministries in the German government, which was held at Wannsee, a suburb of Berlin, in January 1942. No further emigration would be allowed, the amazed bureaucrats were told, because this would simply add to the number of Germany's enemies abroad. Therefore, all Jews within Germany's reach were to be sent to Poland where they would be enslaved and starved. Any survivors would receive "special treatment" to prevent retaliation against Germany. Adolf Eichmann watched the shocked undersecretaries with contempt as they stood around the fireplace after the meeting with drinks in their hands and did not make a word of protest.

Laporterie now began building contacts with men and women he trusted in Pau, Toulouse, Lyon and other cities in Vichy France, as well as in Paris. Among the people in Pau were such high-ranking officials as his friend Colinet. Also in Pau he renewed his friendship with the delightful Henri Vinet, an eloquent man with a lighthearted view of life. In Toulouse, Laporterie worked with a Colonel Weill,[3] a French Jew, a tough and vengeful man. He also worked with a Colonel Riveil, a courageous officer who escaped a Gestapo sweep by fleeing over the mountains to Spain with his lover. He began carrying messages for these men as he traveled about, which was a vital chore at the time, as mail, telegraph and telephones were all suspect. He also kept an eye open for commercial opportunities to support his stores. They needed textiles, clothing, all kinds of small items such as buttons and thread, for the wartime scarcities were getting worse with each passing month.

Laure and Irène, with the help of Laure's mother, Mme Olympe Guilhem, were keeping things going, but at the cost sometimes of bartering their stock for food, which was strictly forbidden. All transactions had to be recorded in monetary terms, including invoices and receipts, so that the Vichy government could impose its taxes. Tax evasion was widespread in the free zone because the government overall was unpopular, despite the popularity of Marshal Pétain. The Vichy French suffered from the illusion, usual in badly governed autocracies, that the leader is a good person surrounded by bad advisers. Tax evasion combined the irresistible lure of personal advantage with a satisfying sense of public duty, for a blow against Vichy was also a blow against Hitler.

In 1941 Raoul Laporterie had helped a Jewish merchant named Zavidowics to cross the line with some cartons of clothes. While Zavidowics went looking for a place to live and do business, Laporterie stored the goods in the hallway and dining room of his apartment in Grenade. This was dangerous because he was supposed to report to the authorities all excess stocks of clothing, and he could not do so without revealing his relationship with Zavidowics.

The Laporteries were thus exposed to trouble that came clothed in the uniforms of police from Pau.

They came into his apartment without knocking, two big uniformed men who refused even to give their names or their reason for coming. Two more walked into the ready-made-clothing store where they accosted Laporterie's nephew, eighteen-year-old Pierrot. Two others went at the same time to the house of a cousin, Mme Veuve Proeres, a road contractor.

In the ready-made-clothing store, the police terrorized the young man, grabbing him by the coat, shouting and snarling at him.

"Who are you? A Jew?"

"No, I'm not."

"No? What about your parents? Your grandparents?"

"No."

"Are you alone? Where's your mother?"

"My mother is dead."

"Your father?"

"He's a prisoner of war in Germany."

"Never mind that — we don't care. Tell us where you hid the merchandise if you want to sleep in your bed tonight. Tell us the truth. If not, you'll find yourself in prison in Pau."

"But we don't have anything."

"Yes, you do. You have eight cartons of merchandise belonging to M. Raoul Laporterie."

"I don't know anything about that at all. I'm just a salesman. Come, you can see for yourself."

Across the street in the dry-goods store, the police neither identified themselves nor even greeted Laporterie's mother-in-law, Mme Guilhem, sixty-seven, or his daughter, Irène, now twenty. Laporterie described the scene later in a letter of protest to the government:

> The policeman opened a cupboard on the landing, pulled out some bars of chocolate that we were about to send to my brother who is a prisoner of war in Germany and a few bottles of an aperitif that we'd had for a long time and were saving. The policeman sneered when they saw these things and said, "You say you have nothing?
>
> My mother-in-law was then interrogated. "So you're hiding merchandise."
>
> "You see for yourselves we are not," she said.
>
> "If you don't tell the truth, you're going to prison tonight."
>
> "I don't think so," she said. "I have nothing to reproach myself for at my age."
>
> "Age doesn't matter," one of the policemen said. "I've already locked up a father of seven children."

Irène was physically small but courageous like her father. As the policemen charged upstairs, looking for what they would not say, opening cupboards, turning out drawers, she demanded so loudly that they say why they were there that one of them finally relented.

"Black-market goods," he said. Irène said they did not sell items on the black market, but he held up the chocolate and the bottles of Armagnac. He said that they were forbidden, so why were they there? Irène replied that they were for her uncle, the POW. She might have said this with a certain emphasis that they didn't like, because it implied that at least her family had been trying to defend the country, while these police were harassing honest storekeepers.

Downstairs the police eventually discovered in plain sight what they had been looking for ever since they had come in: the many boxes of textiles, shirts, trousers and other clothing that Mme Olympe Guilhem, the proprietor, had not declared as required under the law. Irène pointed out that these boxes were not their property, and therefore not for sale. They were standing in plain view and marked Zavidowics, because they belonged to the Mont-de-Marsan merchant who had asked Raoul Laporterie to store them here. Irène said that Zavidowics was in the meantime looking for premises to open a new store.

The police didn't want to be bothered carting all the evidence away, so they sealed each carton with black wax imprinted with the police stamp, then sealed even the door of the dining room, where they had shifted the boxes. "We'll show you what the National Revolution is all about," one of them said. They were referring to Pétain's quasi-religious revolution to rid France of the faults he had decided had led to her downfall, including sensuality, which Pétain publicly condemned. (In private, it was rumored, he romped happily with his young mistress.) The implication for the Laporteries was absurd: they must obey God's laws, which rationed clothes according to the Holy point system.

As they were leaving, the policeman, a local man from Geaune, who knew his Landais, added, "And no convenient fires, you understand?"

A few days later when Laporterie returned to Grenade in secret, he calmed down the angry women, then wrote a coolly articulate letter to the préfecture at Pau, where he still had friends:

The two policemen at Mme Guilhem's searched to the bottom of everything, finding nothing. One of them remarked, "I was sure she had something here."

They then went to Bascons, five kilometers away, where I am mayor, and went into an apartment, to the astonishment of the tenants, saying in a nasty tone of voice, "We're here looking for the cartons of merchandise belonging to M. Laporterie." Still looking for the imaginary goods, the police climbed a ladder to peer through a window into an apartment belonging to the *curé* of Bascons, where they thought they'd find my things. It was crazy.

Laporterie protested the "outrageous attitude of the police, their brutality and the excesses, which scared a lot of people and came near to discrediting" his business and himself, while he was totally innocent of all wrongdoing. He demanded stiffly of *Monsieur le directeur* in the Vichy government that such police practices stop and that the government realize the damage that might have been done to his reputation, and that this painful affair be ended so that he and his family could work honestly and in peace, which was all they wanted. He demanded justice — and the use of his dining room.

Justice was slowly not done. Laporterie hired his friend Larroquette from Mont-de-Marsan to act as his lawyer. The affair dragged on for almost two years, during which Mme Guilhem died, Hitler's armies were defeated at Stalingrad and M. Zavidowics dropped out of sight. For several months the guilty boxes remained in the sealed dining room, which the Laporteries couldn't use. Laporterie and Larroquette had to pester the police at Pau to come and take them away so the family could use the room again. Late in 1942, while the British and Americans were rolling up the last bits of the French empire in North Africa, the remnant of French government at Vichy was sending out able-bodied men to collect dangerous boxes of underwear from a hallway in Grenade.

By the spring assizes of 1943, the prosecution lawyers had decided that because Mme Guilhem was already dead, no case could be made against her, and that because Zavidowics was a Jew in flight, no further punishment could be inflicted on him. So that there would be no conviction, and therefore no fine or humiliation, Larroquette gradually levered the responsibility away from Mme Guilhem and onto Laporterie, for whom he was sure he could get an acquittal. To the right people at Pau he subtly emphasized Laporterie's role as a Resistance hero and savior of the flag. The plan worked. Laporterie was acquitted on grounds of his vaguely defined probity. The newspaper *La République* in Pau reported he had been acquitted because of his "good faith." The editors of *La République* did not know that Laporterie was printing a clandestine newspaper on their presses at night, using their precious paper to attack them for their cowardly toadying to the Germans.

Just as Zavidowics was an innocent man judged guilty, so Laporterie was a guilty man judged innocent. For he and his family were in fact selling goods illegally — without invoices — as were all their fellow merchants, because the Vichy government no longer commanded loyalty or respect among the self-reliant people of Landes.

Zavidowics's goods were confiscated by the state, then consigned to a liquidator, from whom Laporterie nervily tried to buy them back later on.

Larroquette grandly wrote to Laporterie as the trial concluded successfully:

I really regretted not having found you last Sunday at Grenade. Your saleswoman must have given you the papers I left for you. If Zavidowics was not in the occupied zone (in hiding), you would certainly today be in jail. . . . I've asked your saleswoman if you have any raincoats in gabardine for men. I was told you might be able to find one for me between now and June 1. And would you have material for flannel pants or knickers or a blazer? Also, do you have summer suits with a blazer? . . . and could you get me 15-20 liters of gasoline, even on the black market?

CHAPTER 8

Vive de Gaulle

LAPORTERIE'S LAST official protection was ripped away from him in November 1942 by the German troops rolling from Mont-de-Marsan through Grenade on their way to Pau. As the Allies invaded French North Africa, Hitler immediately took over the rest of France, hoping to seize the French navy to help defend Europe against a further Allied landing. The last defiant act by the old French regime was the scuttling of their own fleet in harbor; when the Germans arrived, the fleet's guns were sticking uselessly above the water.

Like other Vichy officials, Raoul Laporterie remained just above the German wave, in office but not in power. The Germans took over direction of the whole country, working through Pétain's puppets in Vichy. The Germans could not administer France directly because there simply weren't enough of them. Millions of their young men had already been killed, wounded or captured on the Russian front. Millions were needed to defend North Africa or to keep down the occupied countries, or to maintain the air defenses of Germany, or continue the attacks on Allied convoys in the North Atlantic. They were so short of manpower that no Germans were ever seen in many of the villages around Grenade. At the city of St-Etienne, which is near Le Chambon-sur-Lignon in the zone once ruled by Vichy, the Germans stationed only three men as the occupation force. They did not arrive until March 1943.

France was being administered by a bizarre government, one that had never been elected yet sought to rule in a bastion of democracy. Like a colonial regime, Vichy tyrannized its own citizens for the advantage of their enemies in order to keep itself in power. Colonized, it pretended to rule a colonial empire that was slowly being taken away from it by a patriot it had condemned to death. Riddled with informers protecting criminals, Vichy was ineptly vicious, feebly repressive. Probably no country in Western Europe has ever had such a high official crime rate as France from 1940 through 1943, when the number of criminal investigations rose from 27,528 to 379,405.[1] By 1944 Laporterie was, in the eyes of Berlin or Vichy, a forger, black marketeer, smuggler, accomplice to murder, terrorist, spy and thief. The high crime rate, along with the shortage of manpower, forced the Germans to continue the demarcation line, which provided checkpoints across the country useful for intercepting saboteurs and Resistance fighters.

Soon after the occupation of the southern zone, Laporterie decided he would be wise to hide out in Pau with his dear friend Henri Vinet for a while. When he arrived at Vinet's Hôtel Félix on the rue Valéry-Meunier, a short narrow street in central Pau, Vinet gave him a room with three doors opening into a choice of two staircases, one of which led to a back entrance onto another street.

Vinet was delighted, as he told Laporterie, "to rekindle the flame of friendship even in wartime." He was already deep into the Resistance himself, as he had been from the beginning. "For me it was perfectly normal," he said. "It was like thirst — it just sprang up by itself. I knew you'd be in it too." He laughed.

That was how it was with all of them.

Vinet and Laporterie began meeting occasionally with British officers to brief them on what was going on in France. This information was very important, but the serious British, who had risked their lives to cross the mountains into France, where they lived next door to death every day, could not at first understand the attitude of Vinet and Laporterie, who saw themselves as actors in a dangerous comedy. To Laporterie and Vinet it was wildly funny when Laporterie received in the mail a report on troop movements in Mont-de-Marsan and Bordeaux, written by Friquet and posted in an envelope that had been stamped PASSED by the censors in Mont-de-Marsan, beneath which was written in tiny letters, "Censored by me — AO."

In 1941, to keep up the spirits of others as they kept up their own, Laporterie and Vinet helped to print a clandestine newspaper on the presses of *La République* in Pau. The motto they chose for the Petites Ailes was Napoleon's "To live in defeat is to die every day." They had planned it as a weekly, but only two issues were published, one on July 1, 1941, the next on July 16. Then Albert Weill of the Resistance in Toulouse asked Laporterie to help with another paper.

He took the train to Toulouse, 250 kilometers to the northeast, to see Weill, an officer in the newly formed network named Franc Tireur.

The Toulouse Laporterie had known was not there when he got off the train. Where there had once been animated people smiling, kissing, honking horns, driving horses on streets shaded by plane trees in front of the rosy-red brick facades of graceful old buildings, there were now empty squares patroled by police. As Laporterie's fellow resister Jean Rivalin wrote:

Toulouse the beautiful, Toulouse the flower, was a dead city, left to the police who stood ready to suppress any demonstration. If I had a heavy heart it was because I have left my family and my friends . . . but also because Toulouse, the pearl of our southwest, capital of sport and song, seemed to me today empty and dead. Liberty was gone, taking with her the joy of life.[2]

Weill was bitter. He had been a chief of militia (*commandant d'armes*) at Grenade until he was denounced. He was convinced that he had been betrayed only because he was Jewish. As soon as the war ended he swore to Laporterie, "I'll kill the son of a bitch who denounced me."

Weill was now directing espionage against the Germans, as well as planning and executing terrorist attacks and publishing his clandestine newspaper called *Franc Tireur*. He knew he was asking a lot when he told Laporterie he wanted him to distribute the newspaper, which was strongly communist.[3] Laporterie had an unpleasant choice: to risk his life partly for an ideology he despised, or to let down France, and Weill, whom he deeply respected. Like most French resisters, he put aside peacetime politics in the name of liberating the country. He agreed.

Weill was glad that Laporterie accepted because the work demanded ingenuity as well as courage. One *réseau* in Toulouse, headed by Charles Wittenberg, a Jewish refugee from Poland, worked out an ingenious system for putting their propaganda newspaper right into the hands of the Germans, among them the soldiers of the famous Das Reich division, which was perhaps the most powerful fighting unit in the world. This division had just returned seriously weakened from the fighting in Russia, so they might be demoralized by astute propaganda. Wittenberg waited until the weather was right, then he and his people hurried to rooftops all over Toulouse. Under the orange-red tiles of the roofs they stuck German-language copies of their paper, leaving them loose enough that when the wind blew the next morning, the papers flew off the roofs all over the city, to the amazement of the Germans who saw propaganda leaflets descending from a sky empty of planes.

By early 1943, Allied propaganda was having a significant effect on the French. The BBC and *Franc Tireur* and the *Courrier de l'Air*, a small newspaper parachuted in from England that Laporterie also distributed, were able to announce victories that seemed all the more impressive because they came at the end of a long series of defeats. At Stalingrad in Russia, the Red Army, for which the Germans had only contempt, stopped General Paulus's advance, encircled his army, then destroyed it. The British, whom the Germans had thought were irrelevant, had defeated Rommel in North Africa. The RAF and the USAF were making devastating attacks on Germany itself. The U-boat campaign in the North Atlantic, which was supposed to choke Britain into submission, was now so costly that soon Grand Admiral Karl Doenitz would order it abandoned. Even in Toulouse these defeats were evident in the worn faces of soldiers just back from the front, or the fear in the eyes of the ones who had just been ordered there. The Resistance, slowly becoming organized, was making direct attacks on German buildings, which were now being protected by armed sentries in front of windows screened by heavy metal mesh against terrorist bombs. Reprisals were growing more frequent: for every German killed the Germans shot or deported many French people seized at random in the jails.

The ambivalence the Germans had shown toward the French from the beginning was now losing its fairer face. At first the Germans had hoped to profit from their conquest while making friends with the French. Hitler returned the ashes of Napoleon's son to the Panthéon as a goodwill gesture, but he refused to return as promised the million and a half prisoners of war he was using as slave labor in Germany. The Germans did not seem to realize that they would not be liked by people they were hurting. "A great number of Frenchmen are highly suspect," reported a German journalist with offended dignity. "They should not be trusted at all. In our magnanimity, our courtesy, our friendship or our politeness, these Frenchmen see only our weakness."[4]

A German soldier in Mont-de-Marsan once asked out Laporterie's friend and post-office employee Renée Darriet, a very attractive young woman. She refused, explaining that she had to take care of her mother who was sick. That night, the

German soldier noticed her sitting in a café having a drink with a Frenchman. The soldier was enraged. He shouted at her so angrily that she was afraid he was going to arrest her. He demanded to know why she would go out with this Frenchman and not with him. Was it because he was German? She managed to calm him down, but she still did not go out with him.

A similar ambivalence afflicted the Germans in their policy toward the Jews. Inflicting pain on the Jews pained many of the Germans themselves, including officers at the highest level. Heinrich Himmler, the head of the SS, which was in charge of the extermination camps, called Hitler's orders to exterminate Jews "a horrid assignment . . . most dreadful . . . and most awful. . . . "[5] Adolf Eichmann, too, said he was shocked when told of Hitler's decision to "physically exterminate the Jews." Eichmann said, "I now lost everything, all joy in my work, all initiative, all interest. Hitler's ally Benito Mussolini was also slow to cooperate with Nazi racism. His government protected refugees and Jews in Italy and in Italian-occupied France, despite pressure from the Germans to join them in the Final Solution.

Occasionally when André Trocmé, Protestant pastor of a village in the Haute-Loire, answered his phone, a mysterious voice with a German accent warned him that there would be a raid soon to round up the Jews whom Trocmé was helping to protect. How did the German know whom to phone? He knew because he was in the German army and charged with rounding up Jews, a job he despised.[6] Every German responsible for tracking or killing innocent people lived in an insoluble quandary. The natural sense of identification between human beings, which may be suppressed but not eradicated, meant that every obedient German carrying out these "most awful" orders felt something of the pain he was inflicting. This was the "animal pity" in Hannah Arendt's words, which the SS commanders tried to eradicate by praising and rewarding "toughness." This same obedient German, therefore, oscillated between identification with his victim, which he could not eliminate, and hatred for his victim. The victim also served to remind the German of the dreadful punishment he himself would suffer if he were ever caught. The Nazi also saw, with a vicarious thrill of fear as if he were watching a horror movie, the drama of his own punishment. Hence the strange swings of German behavior — for instance, the pistol jammed up against Farbos's nose succeeded immediately by an amiable offer of a cigarette. Thus the German voice warning Trocmé on the phone, followed soon by the trucks, perhaps sent there by the same voice.

Pastor Trocmé's clearly saying to the Germans, and to Vichy officials bewildered by this Frenchman's protest, "Yes, we have Jews here, but we will not give them up to you," was doing exactly what Solzhenitsyn called on everyone to do in the face of tyranny. "Just one refusal to grovel, one such show of moral courage from all the slaves among us, is all that is needed; we could take a single breath and be free. But we dare not." That this has at least a chance to work was proven not only by Solzhenitsyn's amazing personal success in Russia, revealing the truth about prison camps, but also by the nonviolent campaign of Gandhi against the British in India.

But the Landais are quite unlike the Calvinist Protestants of Le Chambon or the courageously uncompromising Solzhenitsyn or the quietist Hindus who followed Gandhi. The Landais say of themselves with rueful amusement, "Nous sommes malins," meaning they are naughty though not vicious, like rambunctious boys. The smiling guile with which Laporterie protected himself protected his passengers as well as his fellow Basconnais. In the end it also protected the Germans to some degree, because if they had been openly defied in 1941 or 1942, they would probably have begun committing atrocities like those they committed in 1944 in Oradour, Tulle and Grenade, making all France thirst for the savage revenge that was to come.

The impudent Laporterie may have elicited some ambivalent sympathy from the Germans in Mont-de-Marsan. Certainly Gestapo commander Friedrich Dohse far away in Bordeaux no longer trusted his subordinates in Mont-de-Marsan, because they failed so often to get their man. Soon after the Germans occupied the free zone of France, he ordered that all arrests normally made by the Gestapo or police of Mont-de-Marsan be henceforth turned over to the Gestapo in Auch, in the next *département* to the east — Gers. He was hoping to stop the leak in the headquarters at Mont-de-Marsan.

Of the 250,000 Jews in France who were saved, mainly by their compatriots, probably the great majority were installed by mid-1943 in safe houses with new identities — like the five new Greniers in Lestelle-Betharram. This was mainly because of the resistance of the French people to the official anti-Semitism of the Vichy government, which had never been elected or submitted to a referendum. In the *département* of Puy-de-Dôme in central France, for example, this passive resistance saved many Jews from deportation during the first big Vichy roundup in August 1942, when more than fifty percent evaded seizure with the help of their friends. Every roundup from then on was less effective, because secretaries in offices refused to type out the lists of names, or because Red Cross officials phoned out warnings, or individual policemen notified refugees before taking part in raids on empty houses. A raid in Puy-de-Dôme in February 1943 netted fewer than ten percent of its target; by September 1943 the savior system was so effective that 273 of 286 on the list of foreign Jews escaped, as well as 162 of 170 native-born.[7]

The newest class of refugees coming to the Laporteries, Vinets and Tachons was young men fleeing the STO (Service du Travail Obligatoire), which was a forced-labour program. Announced in 1943, it was intended to alleviate the shortage of armaments workers in Germany by supplying millions of French workers. Because the Germans knew that young

Raoul's mother, Anne Laporterie, about 1887

Paul Laporterie and his son Raoul, during the First World War

Raoul in winter gear during the First World War

Raoul from a postcard sent in 1918 to Laure Guilhem, during his imprisonment in Germany

Wedding photo of Raoul Laporterie and Laure Guilhem, July 3, 1919

Souvenir postcard of the course landaise, *which Raoul helped to organize on October 22, 1939, to benefit the Alsatian refugees who had arrived in the region.*

Street in Grenade-sur-l' Adour about 1920

Sauteur *leaping over a bull during a* course landaise

A bullfight in Mont-de-Marsan

Raoul's Ausweis *permitting him to cross the frontier between Mont-de-Marsan and Grenade-sur-l'Adour*

Raoul's false identity card in the name of Raymond Cazenave issued in November 1942

Ici est tombé
René VIELLE
"Mort pour la FRANCE"
le 13 Juin 1944

RENE VIELLE
LA RESISTANCE
DE SUR ADOUR
AL SOUVENIR

Abel Oppenheimer, who became one of Raoul's best friends during his enforced stay in Mont-de-Marsan

Monument to René Vielle, Resistance leader at Grenade-sur-l'Adour, who was shot during an attack on the Germans on June 13, 1944

Members of the Maquis at Grenade-sur-l'Adour, photographed after the liberation in 1945

Laure Laporterie, about 1946

Caricature of Raoul, undated

*The Laporterie family in the 1950s. Back row: Roger and Irène Duvignau, Laure and Raoul Laporterie.
Front row: Nicole Duvignau, Martine Proëre, Annie Duvignau*

The Cassuto sisters stand on either side of American writer Peter Hellman and Raoul after the planting of the commemorative carob tree, Avenue of the Righteous, Yad Vashem, Jerusalem, July 8, 1980

PETER HELLMAN

Raoul receives the Médaille de combattant volontaire at Mont-de-Marsan, 1981

LAPORTERIE ARCHIVES

ELISABETH BACQUE

C'EST CONTRE CE MUR
QUE LE 13 JUIN 1944
DES OTAGES FURENT
RASSEMBLES ET DEPORTES
CEUX DONT LES NOMS
SONT GRAVES
ONT DONNE LEUR VIE
POUR LA FRANCE

BRETHES   ANDRE
CASTELNAU GABRIEL
DAUGE   JEAN
HARTE   CYPRIEN
LABURTHE   EDOUARD
LERICHE   JOSEPH
LIMON   RENE
PARISOT   FIACRE
RICAU   PIERRE
TAUZIEDE   LOUIS
ULRICH   CLAUDE

SOUVENONS NOUS

Monument on the wall of the mairie of Grenade-sur-l'Adour to the hostages deported to Dachau on June 13, 1944

Main square in Grenade-sur-l'Adour, 1983

Mairie in Bascons, 1983

André Tachon, Raoul and author Jim Bacque in Grenade-sur-l'Adour, 1983

La Petite Maison in Grenade-sur-l'Adour as it is today

Raoul speaks after receiving the Légion d'honneur from Jean Cuvelier, préfet of Landes (left) on January 15, 1989. Claude Cazalis, mayor of Bascons, on the right

Raoul pins the *Médaille de combattant volontaire* on André Tachon

André and Magda Trocmé and their four children, Le Chambon-sur-Lignon

Gathering of friends and family after the Légion d'honneur presentation. Back row: M. Lefrere, president of the Anciens Combattants du Canton, Gwenaëlle Houdy, Mapy Lalanne, Nicole Houdy, Maylis Houdy, Raoul. Front row: Jean Larrieu, former mayor of Mont-de-Marsan, Mme de Chiabrando, Laure Laporterie

Frenchmen could not want to work in Germany, they offered to return to France one POW for every three workers who did go. Foreseeing, too, that the French would ignore this offer to sell them the same pig twice, they announced harsh penalties for evading STO or for helping anyone to evade it. The result was equally foreseeable: large numbers of young Frenchmen fled the country for Spain or fled to the *maquis*, which is a Corsican word for "wooded highlands." By September 1943 Vichy knew that over 600,000 young Frenchmen nominally eligible for the labor draft were officially "in default or presumed to be," or else were exempted by sympathetic officials like Laporterie. For every two young men who actually went to Germany at least seven fled, along with many of the Vichy police themselves, who were disgusted by the new policy.

So many fled to the bush that the Resistance movement itself now began to be known as the Maquis. The favorite terrain of the Maquis was the high country of central France, where they could hide in the woods or isolated farms. The Germans had anticipated that the order would be unpopular, but perhaps they had not fully understood what they were creating: a class of young "criminals" whose self-interest coincided with patriotism. These men had nothing to lose now. The armies of the Resistance were drafted into being by the desperation of the Germans.

Young men came to Laporterie, Tachon and Vinet for help. Vinet and Laporterie began a taxi service to a *passeur* they knew in the high Pyrénées. Day after day they fabricated papers, stole gasoline and drove young dodgers up to the Hôtel Bidegain at Mauléon in the mountains. Hoping to get to North America but lacking English, many of them, like young Jean Gauthier of Grenade, claimed to be Canadian. So many bizarre refugees were crossing the mountains now that not much surprised the Spanish police anymore. One refugee from Bordeaux who asked Laporterie for papers said he was an Iroquois seaman who had been stranded in Bordeaux in 1940.

Some of the young men fleeing from the north seeking Laporterie by reputation wound up in Aire with Tachon who was now running the Hôtel du Commerce there. Tachon was once again in a difficult position because eight rooms in his hotel had been requisitioned by officers of the Hermann Goering Panzer division, which was resting. People were suddenly tense in Aire, because the local Resistance had attacked a shipment of planes leaving the Bréguet factory in Aire, destroying in this and later attacks almost two dozen planes. Everyone in Aire was apprehensive about Resistance attacks and German reprisals when two young Frenchmen came in one day asking Tachon for help in joining the Maquis. Tachon said he didn't think there were any Maquis in the region and that even if he knew how to help the two men, which he didn't, he wouldn't help anyone, let alone a couple of strangers coming in with such a preposterous request. The young men lounged about the pretty little town for several days, confirming Tachon's suspicion that they feared nothing from the local police or from the German troops.

After a week, they skipped out without paying their bill, which they would not have done if the Germans or Vichy had hired them, so Tachon was left wondering about them, as well as paying their debts. He continued helping real refugees join the Maquis, which was swarming in the hills that stretch from Aire south to the mountains.

Many of his refugees Tachon sent on to Vinet and Laporterie, who already had their hands full. So many people were trying to climb the Pyrénées to get out of France in those days that to have a knapsack on your back was to risk immediate arrest.

Returning from the mountains in his car early one humid morning, Vinet noticed people staring oddly at him. Some were laughing and pointing. He stopped the car and got out to look. Someone had scrawled "Vive de Gaulle" in the dewy dust. Hastily he rubbed it out. He got back into the car, shaken.

Who had done this? Why? He couldn't think of answers, but

the questions wouldn't go away. Normally a jocular man, Vinet couldn't shrug off this incident because it made him feel as if his head were framed in a sniper's sights. He had never been nervous face-to-face with the Germans, but now he could not stop worrying. He knew he was being watched by someone who could denounce him to the Gestapo at any moment.

CHAPTER 9

The Joy of Goodness

THE FAMOUS historian Henri Amouroux, who devoted a section to Raoul Laporterie in one of his books, quoted an anonymous poem from the French Revolution,[1] which applied to the way Laporterie and millions of other French people who had to live by their wits and bizarre trading, in 1943:

> La fureur de l'agiotage
> A métamorphosé les gens
> Le cordonnier vend des rubans
> Et la coiffeuse du fromage
>
> Partout l'agioteur s'exerce
> Pour tromper à bon escient
> Enfin tout le monde commerce
> Excepté le négociant.

This translates from the French of 1795 roughly as follows:

> When greed's in conflict with ideals
> Service to profit sometimes kneels
> So dentists bank and doctors write
> And lawyers option wine by night.

But if we say it's no disgrace
To make a buck in the marketplace
We'll all get into trade and then
There'll be no need for businessmen.

Like a revolutionary, Laporterie was living on the edge. He moved dozens of times a year, in and out of Pau, Toulouse, Lyon, Grenade, Bascons, even Paris, usually under his own name, sometimes as Raymond Casenave. Here he was Raoul, there he was Agent 33 (in the *réseau* later known as Maître René Vielle). In his suitcase at various times were contraband coffee, illegal newspapers, black-market tobacco, refugee diamonds, smuggled gold, dubious textiles and roast pork to bribe a German.

M. and Mme Lamothe, Jewish refugees from Bordeaux whom he had helped cross years earlier, were caught in the free zone by the Nazis who put them in the notorious camp in Gurs near Pau. Hannah Arendt, who was imprisoned here, discovered the "banality of evil" in places like Gurs. But even in abominable Gurs people were kind to one another. Hélène Rott de Neufville, a French Quaker, went in with other volunteers to help the prisoners. When one of the deportation trains was being loaded despite the protests of the Quakers, she stood with tears in her eyes outside one of the cars saying goodbye to her friends. "When they saw me there," she said, "they started throwing things out the windows to me, letters, notes attached to necklaces, rings, whatever they had, with addresses for me to send these things on to their relatives." De Neufville stood there trying to catch them all, until there were so many that she simply held out her skirt to the rolling train while the last words fell in.[2]

The Lamothes escaped from the camp at Gurs, then ran to Laporterie at Bascons, who put them up in his house there. They were denounced to the police, who arrested them again. M. Lamothe was sent to the *camp de représailles* (punishment camp) at Muret in the neighboring *département* of Haute-Garonne, while his wife was left free for the moment. She went to Laporterie, who said he would see what he could do.

It is easy to imagine him on that October afternoon driving the Juvaquatre too fast up the steep winding streets of Aire to the plateau, where one sees the first view of Pau against the gray Pyrénées. He is figuring out a route through the hampering bureaucracy as adroitly as he drives — which will probably be almost as dangerous. He is absolutely singleminded in his determination to get Lamothe out. Nothing will stop him because he knows the man's life is at stake. It excites him to live so intensely, concentrated on a need so great that it excludes everything else. This is where he likes to live, on this edge of hope.

He might talk to someone at the camp, or perhaps he should have a word with his old friend Colinet, an important official in the *préfecture* at Pau. He has heard that an escape tunnel is being built by the prisoners at Gurs; perhaps he could get Lamothe transferred in time to make a break. A Resistance group has somehow been smuggling members into the camp to get news, bring out papers and so on. Would such a group, which might be known to Colonel Weill of Toulouse, help get Lamothe out?

As he thinks about his problem, he pays no attention to the fact that because his passengers, the Lamothes, were denounced he is automatically in more danger himself. In his ambition he has made envious enemies, who might like to scrawl "Vive de Gaulle" on the trunk of the Juvaquatre one morning.

He enters Colinet's office with a cheerful greeting. *"Bonjour, mon capitaine. Comment allez-vous? Comment va votre mère? Et belle-mère? Et les enfants? Et madame?"* Solicitous inquiries pour from him, his face all smiling interest. He has all the time in the world for Captain Colinet, who feels better as soon as Laporterie comes into the room. Laporterie looks so good — some people might say he is beautiful — that sometimes strangers have the impression at first that he is wearing makeup. Colinet smiles back. He cannot help but be pleased at the visit, although he suspects it may bring him trouble.

Laporterie's sympathy has a special Landais overtone, as if all the *petit pays* of Landes were one big family, with cousins all over France. Reminded, Colinet thinks affectionately of his own dear relatives — his "beautiful cousin Jeanne," his "charming sympathetic wife," his "sainted mother," his "distinguished father," his two "beautiful children," whose names, ages and illnesses Laporterie remembers so well that it is impossible for Colinet, feeling loved and cherished, to feel anything but loving and cherishing. Colinet begins to feel better about his life. He does not live just to arrest black marketeers, play the fine line between the Resistance and Vichy, get ahead in the bureaucracy, put his hands on a goose for Sunday noon. He was born for more than this. He is worth more than this. Laporterie reminds him of what that more of life is — the lives of others. He mentions what a *"brave type"* Lamothe is, and how shamefully he has been treated along with so many others who are separated from their families through no fault of their own, to suffer in dirty cold camps where the food is abominable, in fear of deportation and death.

Colinet begins to feel a shamed admiration for this dapper man who is risking his skin for someone he hardly knows, while he, Colinet, is sitting in his safe seat looking out his tall window over the vineyards of Jurançon to the mountains. He has become something he does not want to be — a danger to Raoul Laporterie. Yet Laporterie is giving him the chance to make his life worth living.

Neither bribed nor flattered, neither threatened nor cajoled, Colinet picks up the pen to sign the letter that will save the lives of two people he doesn't know, who mysteriously have become part of his family. He may wonder at himself later, but at this moment, there is nothing else he can do but sign. That is all Laporterie needs.

Lamothe was released soon after. He rejoined his wife, then came to thank Laporterie. Having passed unscathed through the system, overjoyed to be reunited, they felt that at last it would be safe to accept Laporterie's invitation to return to his house in Bascons.

Yet, on October 12, 1943, the police were again at their door, which the Lamothes kept locked. It was the only door to the house, so they ran up to the attic, scrambled out a skylight, slithered down the tile roof onto a veranda, then ran through the fields to hide in the pine woods bordering the fields.

The police spread the word through the village that a deportation order had been issued against the two Jews. Anyone sheltering them would share their fate. A concentration camp.

Two of the bakers in town, Messrs Meispleigt and Gourdun, found them hiding in the woods. For nine days they sheltered them in a house they owned together while Dumartin made new papers and Laporterie looked for a safer house.

Late in the evening of October 21, Laporterie boldly drove into Bascons to pick up the Lamothes. He chauffeured them to a new safer house unknown to the police.

As the war grew worse for the Germans in Russia, Sicily, the Atlantic, even in their own cities, the defeated peoples of Europe took hope. They began to fight again. The Germans hurried to rid Europe of the annoying minorities while they still had the power. They fought skillfully against the resisters, especially in France. It was about then that Sarah Yaeche in Lestelle-Betharram heard that her parents had been deprived of their furniture by the police in Bordeaux under new racist legislation. Before they could bring themselves to believe what was about to happen, they were arrested. With many hundreds of children who had been seized under orders by Maurice Papon, a general secretary in the city administration of Bordeaux, they were sent in a cattle car to the huge transfer camp at Drancy, where the trains were assembled to go to the concentration camps in the east.[3] As the French writer Michel Slitinsky wrote after the war:

How is one to understand the savage expedition sent to a farm near Mont-de-Marsan where, with an escort of field-police, six mercenaries captured Robert Melendes, eleven years old, who was baby-sitting five "illegal" children: the blonde Monique Ciolek who had just celebrated her third birthday; Jacqueline Mostekowitch and Salomon Szarc, five years, Hélène Gutter and Bernard Edelstein, seven years, all of them sent that morning of the 18th August, 1942, to the camp at Merignac? The list of internees had grown at an insane pace since the end of July. On the 28th, thirty-four persons including children were arrested at Orthez and Libourne, on the 29th sixteen at St-Palais and thirty-one at Mont-de-Marsan . . .[4]

In the same few days that Laporterie was extricating the Lamothes from the police, Friedrich Dohse in Bordeaux sent his Gestapo against the *réseau* Ceux de Notre-Dame-de-Castille, to which Mlle Renée Darriet and her brother, of Mont-de-Marsan, both belonged. As soon as Mlle Darriet heard her brother had been arrested, not far from where she was in Bordeaux, she hurried back to the post office in Mont-de-Marsan to telephone warnings to the other members of the *réseau*. This would also warn off the members of Libé Nord, a *réseau* to which they had ties, and in which Laporterie had also worked.

She was arrested, taken to Fort-du-Ha, where Laporterie vainly tried to get her released. But her crime was far too serious for his influence. She was interrogated, tortured, convicted, then sent by cattle car to Ravensbruck concentration camp in northeast Germany, along with Charles de Gaulle's niece Geneviève.

The women at Ravensbruck were used by Nazi doctors experimenting with treatments for battlefield infections. Fritz Fisher and Ludwig Stumpfegger cut open the women, stuffed wood shavings, dirt, glass, streptococcus, staphylococcus and gangrene cultures into the wound, then sewed them up again. They also attempted to transplant bones and muscles from one patient to another. The women who survived were horribly maimed.

Renée's brother was sent to Buchenwald.

Laporterie whirled around France on money supplied by the Resistance, which came from donations by friends or members, or from robberies. There was also a supply of counterfeit currency printed in England, then dropped by parachute at night onto fields designated by code messages over the BBC. Laporterie received help all through the war from Laure and Irène, in Grenade, who wrote to him using a false name. One letter from Irène in 1943 reads in part:

Dear Sir:

How are you? The time must seem to you long, but be patient and wait calmly. A man came by to give me the green box which you will find in the mail. Everyone at home is fine. Our village is just the same.

Today all men's bicycles were requisitioned. Twenty were taken, among them Mouchez's, which we had been using for the house.

The weather is terrible, the days seem endless. I don't know yet if we can get tobacco, but as soon as we do get some, we'll send it to you. Business goes well, but I think that for the moment we'd better sell off inventory and slow down new purchasing. I hope soon to have the pleasure of seeing you.

In the meantime I embrace you very affectionately.

Irène, who signed herself Kiki, was feeling circumspect partly because a German officer had just been billeted with them. He slept in the big double bed where Laporterie had been born. Every day he went to Mont-de-Marsan to work, so they were left in peace for dinner at noon.

These dinners became famous, for Laure was very hospitable in true Landais style, always sharing her food and her cooking. From their land in Bascons came pigs and vegetables, from Raoul's scrounging trips came bolts of cloth, thread, socks, shirts, all of which Laure or Irène could trade for food. Irène loved to get on her bike and head out into the hills above Grenade toward some isolated farm near Fargue or Classun, where the occupation of France was still only a rumor to *madame* or *monsieur*, who after three years had yet to see a German.

Like her mother and father before her, Irène would tell her news, make her trades, then strap the fresh-killed duck or eggs on the back of the bike, ready for the exciting fast run, with her eyes sprouting tears, back down the long hill through the woods, around the chapel at Notre-Dame-de-Rugby, around the corner, then up over the arched steel bridge across the Adour and, smiling, into the main square of Grenade.

Laure would have half a dozen visitors on most days, each of whom might bring something to contribute to the table. At midday they talked safely about the news from Raoul or his refugees, or the STO. Many of the young men who came to her table had been handed from village to farm, cousin to aunt, escaping the Milice (French police of Vichy), who were hunting them down to put on the labor trains to Germany. These young men looked upon La Petite Maison as a second home where "Mami" Laure cared for them like a mother.

Laporterie went on a mission to Paris to see Poidloué and to pick up a stock of clothing hidden by a friend who had fled to

Laporterie in 1941. Laporterie wangled the use of a truck driven by a friend so they could pick up the clothing. Dressed like a laborer, he traveled in the truck with his friend because it was safer than going by train. Unfortunately they had trouble with the truck, which they had to abandon in Paris just before the curfew. They were walking through the Place de la République at midnight, highly visible in the heavy snow that had just fallen, when a machine gun very close started firing at them. They ran for the corner of a building as bullets smacked into the walls beside them. The Germans who had been firing at them did not follow as they ran to their apartment.

Because Laporterie and Poidlouë had together helped Allied airmen escape from France, it seems likely that they met while Laporterie was in Paris to discuss arrangements for the next lot of airmen. Poidlouë was head of the Paris section of his *réseau*, Les Sauterelles, which was run from Lille, a city famous for its resistance to the Germans. The Gestapo had almost certainly been surveying Poidlouë's apartment in the rue Pallu, because they raided it while Poidlouë and his wife, Julienne, were in it. The couple ran for a back door. The Germans shot at them, hitting Julienne in the chest. She kept on going. They escaped together by train to Mont-de-Marsan, but Julienne was in constant pain. Poidlouë got her by taxi to the Château de Myredé, where she died.

The Darriets and Poidlouës, along with many other friends of Laporterie's, were arrested or killed by the Gestapo in 1943, some of them as a result of the successful work in Bordeaux of Gestapo chief Friedrich Dohse. Dohse was chasing the members of the *réseau* Jade-Amicole, to which Laporterie belonged. This was one of the *réseaux* set up by Colonel Arnould (Olivier) in Bordeaux. Jade-Amicole agents were placed in the Bordeaux tramway system, in the administrative offices responsible for bridges and roads, the local section of the national railway and the gas, water and forest commissions. Friedrich Dohse and his men broke up most of this *réseau* in September 1943, but he

didn't catch either Laporterie or Arnould. Dohse was spectac-
ularly successful, however, with his raid on the head of Section
B of the Armée Secrète in the Bordeaux area.

The Resistance chief, Grandclément, struck a deal with
Dohse: he would give up big stocks of Resistance arms in return
for the freedom of his men. The Gestapo lived up to its promise,
as did many of Grandclément's men. The fierce Léonce Dus-
sarrat, called Léon des Landes, who was the departmental chief
of Les Forces Françaises de l'Intérieur,[5] denounced Grandclément's deal. He broke all connection with the former *réseau*,
ordered his men to shoot Dohse and Grandclément on sight,
then went into hiding in the hills, probably above Grenade.
The movement locally was in confusion, infiltrated, lacking
arms, leaderless.

Laporterie nevertheless went back to Bascons, where he still
functioned as mayor on flying secret visits, signing papers in a
hurry, giving the faithful Dumartin instructions, then disap-
pearing. On one visit, he wrote a letter defending a teacher in
Bascons against an order sending him to Germany as a laborer.
The teacher, Galaber, got off, one of many local men saved
from the STO by Laporterie.

Laporterie was in Toulouse some time later, picking up the
copies of *Franc Tireur* for Landes. He took a room in his
customary hotel near the station, using his alias Raymond
Casenave, because he had a meeting in his room that night with
an agent, a woman from the Dordogne. The agents were not
supposed to know one another's names so that they could not
reveal them even under torture. Early in the morning, about
six, the Germans raided the hotel. This was their method of
dealing with the covert opposition of some of the Vichy police,
who pretended to be cooperating with the Germans while
actually protecting the French. In an unannounced raid, or *rafle*
as they called it, the Germans often rounded up in a hotel or a
train station people they wanted.

Two Germans came to the door of Laporterie's room early

in the morning, after the agent from the Dordogne had departed. One of them asked Laporterie his name, then, noticing a history book Laporterie had been reading, picked it up. He talked about the book with Laporterie, then picked up a ring that had been lying on a dresser. He also admired the ring. Laporterie talked amiably to the soldier who seemed bored with his work and eager to make friends. They left. Laporterie quickly packed his suitcase and started down the stairs.

The lobby was crowded with German soldiers and guests. Laporterie started through them to the desk, then remembered with horror that he had given the friendly soldier upstairs his real name, while he had registered under Raymond Casenave, which was the name on his identity papers. These he had left at the desk, as French law required. To get out of the hotel, he would have to pay and claim his papers. If the Germans noticed the falsification, he was certain to be arrested. Once they had their hands on him, he would probably end up before a firing squad or, at the very least, on a train to a camp in Germany.

Should he run? Then he would not get his papers back, and he was far from his seals in Bascons. He decided that he had to brazen it out: if he ran now, then was asked for his papers later in the day, he was certain to be arrested. He walked over to the desk, made polite conversation with the desk clerk while paying his bill, took his papers and walked out among the soldiers. Outside, the guests coming out of the hotel were being inspected by soldiers. The friendly one was among them. Laporterie was stopped by a strange soldier asking for papers, but the friendly one said, "Oh, he's all right. Let him through. We already checked him upstairs." Laporterie walked through.

He took a load of *Franc Tireurs* with him back to Pau. The train was crowded as usual, so Laporterie was forced to sit beside a uniformed German. When he swung off the train with his suitcase in his hand to change at Tarbes, the handle broke and the suitcase fell on the concrete platform and burst open, spilling out the illegal papers. Laporterie ran for his life, out of the station, down the street, then disappeared into Tarbes.

Toward the end of 1943, perhaps in early 1944, he was in his usual room in the Hôtel Félix when Vinet came to his room in a hurry. "Quick," he said, "get out. The Germans are here looking for you."

Laporterie started out the second, escape, door, which he had already used several times during *rafles*, but this time Vinet said, "No, they've blocked off the street and the whole *quartier*. You can't get away."

"What can I do?" asked Laporterie.

"This way," said Vinet. "Into the dining room. Sit down and act normal."

Together they went downstairs to the dining room. Vinet had a clientele of German officers who ate regularly at his hotel because the food was good. These men were favored among Germans of the time, because they were the sons of rich influential men who kept them out of the dangerous parts of Hitler's empire, such as the Afrika Korps and the Russian front. These men were stationed in a peaceful part of France with few air raids, lots of wine and enough food.

Vinet approached a table where three uniformed Germans were sitting. He said politely, "Would you mind if this gentleman sat with you? As you can see there is nowhere else to sit."

The Germans, politely speaking good French, made room for Laporterie, who sat down beside them. The inspection went on through the rest of the hotel. When the Gestapo came to the dining room, they glanced in on a peaceful scene of uniformed Germans eating their lunch. They perhaps did not even notice Laporterie; if they did, they must have decided he could not be the man they wanted because he was eating amiably next to three uniformed officers.

After lunch, when the raid was over, Vinet roared with laughter and said, "Did you enjoy your lunch?"

Laporterie was not amused. "It was terrible," he said. "I had no appetite, but I had to eat. Now I can't digest anything."

Laporterie stayed on at the Félix. Not only was he Vinet's contact man for the Réseau d'Azur, he was also protected as he would not be elsewhere. Whenever Laporterie checked in, Vinet wrote his real name in the register but put down an incorrect room number. The police asked for Laporterie by name twice. Each time, Vinet said, "Yes, he's here." Satisfied that Vinet was telling the truth, the police went up the stairs to a vacant room. In the meantime, Vinet or his assistant would warn Laporterie to skip out the back door. When the police came back down, frustrated, Vinet pretended surprise that Laporterie had left without a word to him, without even paying his bill. The police probably concluded that Laporterie had been warned by someone outside the hotel. They did not believe that Vinet was hiding him, because Vinet admitted both times that Laporterie was there.

Vinet teased Laporterie by deliberately placing one of his guests, a pretty young Jewish medical student, in the room next to Laporterie's.

Laporterie felt a strong bond with her. She was a refugee like himself, alone, away from her family, her friends. Like him, she was living a lie, every day in danger of arrest and deportation, all the while having to pretend to live normally.

During a thunderstorm one night, the power failed. The lightning flashed into the rooms; rain and thunder shook the roof tiles. The student ran into Laporterie's room and jumped on his bed. "I'm scared," she said. He sat beside her and stroked her head. They held on to each other.

The next morning, when Laporterie told Vinet the story, Vinet laughed with delight. "And then what happened, Raoul?" he said. "Did you have a lightning rod to protect her?"

CHAPTER 10

Baufübrer Laporterie

New Year's Day 1944 was a time of hopeful suffering for the French. The Germans were in retreat everywhere: in Russia, in Italy, which had gone over to the Allies, and in the skies over Germany itself, which were now dominated by Allied air fleets bombing German cities every night.

These fire-storm raids burned the people in their homes and the factories making armaments. Losses of men throughout Hitler's empire forced the Germans to increase their labor levies in the occupied countries, driving even more young men to sympathetic mayors like Laporterie for papers to free them from slave labor in the burning Ruhr region.

One young man came to him asking to be married, because the mayor of his village, Renung, had refused to perform the ceremony. The mayor apparently believed the young man didn't really want to marry his bride but was only marrying for convenience to avoid the STO, which was illegal. Laporterie, now a law unto himself, hastily married the young couple. "It is better to marry than to burn," said Saint Paul.

Food in the cities of France in 1944 was so hard to find that many people had no time to do anything but work and hunt for something to eat. To the French, who love their food and drink, "marketing in 1943 and 1944 was a daily tragedy," as de Gaulle said. The Germans took about thirteen percent of the meat produced in France.[1] Agricultural production dropped by twenty to thirty percent during the occupation.[2] In the Place Pierre-Laffitte in Bordeaux, the pigeon population fell from the countless thousands, which had lived on the scraps casually dropped by the well-fed Bordelais, down to eighty-five — counted by a journalist scrambling for tidbits in a world that for him, as for pigeons, was mainly distant disasters causing local hardships.

The Landais, whom the Germans had once found easy to get along with, suddenly turned nasty. Trains were bombed, bridges collapsed, wires fell, factories burned. Laporterie whizzed around with his fake papers, reports, maps of German installations to attack, carrying memorized messages from a *réseau* chief to an agent, or false ration cards for refugees. His garage-owning friend in Mont-de-Marsan, Dupeyron, got his hands on detailed plans of the air base in Mont-de-Marsan from an Austrian anti-Nazi officer who worked there. The plans were smuggled out of the forbidden coastal zone, over the demarcation line, then out to England. The plans may have been among papers smuggled out by Laporterie who, like most agents, didn't know what he was carrying unless he had produced it himself. The Allies soon bombed the base to take out the big Focke-Wulf Condors, which were guiding the dangerous new electrosubmarines to Allied convoys. After the raid, one of the Allied planes was shot down in the woods west of Mont-de-Marsan. The pilot bailed out. Uninjured, but unable to speak French, he was found by some boys who took him to Le Penan, the Lemée estate. They buried his clothes and found him new ones, probably provided by La Petite Maison.

This young pilot, whom some people later remembered as Canadian, others as American, touched Mme Lemée with his "unimaginable courage." She gave him a bottle of his favorite cologne, which he had not seen since the beginning of the war. Dupeyron offered to take the pilot in at his apartment in Mont-de-Marsan, which was located over his garage. When the pilot heard that the garage had been requisitioned by the Germans to repair their trucks he was very reluctant to go. To get to the apartment he would have to enter the garage itself and walk in full view of the German soldiers up the stairs to the apartment. Dupeyron told him that the best place to hide was where the enemy does not search — in his own house. He said all the pilot had to do was to walk in as if he did it every day. The pilot went right through the Germans without being identified.

The message asking for help to liberate the pilot went north to the *réseau* in Paris. The Resistance by now was organized on such a scale that downed flyers were regularly flown out by short-takeoff Lysanders of the RAF, which landed on turf fields at night. Allied airpower was so strong that the Luftwaffe could do little against it.

While the pilot waited, Dupeyron suggested that he visit the air base to see what damage he had done. Dupeyron, who had his own pass to the base, had often taken strangers there without being stopped, so he was certain the pilot would be safe. The two of them toured the base in a German truck, observing the big Condors and the effects of the raid. They left without being stopped.

Within two days, the pilot, pretending to be deaf and mute, was on his way north, accompanied by two agents of the Paris network, on a train full of German soldiers going on leave. He flew out safely to England with the report of the effects of the raid.

Laporterie and Vinet helped the Allies on the next assault in the region, this time against the base at Pau. Laporterie, acting as liaison to Vinet's Réseau d'Azur, had been asked by his contact, a British officer, for a plan of the air base at Pau, showing runways, hangars, anti-aircraft gun emplacements and so on, so that the RAF could bomb it effectively. They wanted to take out the anti-aircraft guns first so they could bomb the base without risk to themselves or to French civilians.

Laporterie went to Vinet who was in charge of the canteen at the base.

Vinet could move around fairly freely, except on the runways. But to provide a baseline for the bombers he would have to show the positions of the camouflaged anti-aircraft gun emplacements in relation to these runways.

He and Laporterie studied the problem. The only way for Vinet to get onto the runways was by doing some kind of work. But he was normally confined to the canteen. Then it hit them — when workers were out there, he could take them something to drink.

He saw his chance one warm day when the French civilian workers were at the far end of a runway doing repairs. He loaded up a wheelbarrow with wine, beer, fruit juice and ice, then slowly wheeled it along the side of the runway, measuring the exact locations of the hangars and anti-aircraft gun emplacements by counting his steps. He sold the drinks, came back checking his calculations as he did so, then returned to the hotel to see Laporterie. Putting pencil to paper, he drew a map showing the four compass points, runways, location of anti-aircraft guns and marked the distances in meters. Breaking the rule that all information should be passed orally only, Raoul took the completed map to his British contact, who relayed it to England.

When the RAF arrived over the base, they bombed all the anti-aircraft guns first, then destroyed the hangars, about a dozen parked planes and the control tower of the defenseless base. Not one French civilian was hurt. No British planes were lost.

The bombs that fell on the air bases at Mont-de-Marsan and Pau were the first significant evidence that many people in the southwest of France had seen of the power coming to liberate them.

They were encouraged by the signs everywhere of German breakup, even in Lestelle-Betharram, where Yaeche saw a gray-haired German soldier weeping because he had just been ordered to the Russian front.

In Pau, a Maquis unit boldly attacked the huge stone Bernadotte barracks in the center of the city, where Napoleon had rounded up local farm boys to herd to Russia ahead of him. The Germans in the barracks, dreading the same journey, were completely surprised one night by a Maquis unit flinging grenades, firing Sten guns and bombing their vehicles. Enraged by the sudden defiance of a people that had already been defeated, the Germans rounded up over a thousand suspects that night and during the early morning.

Laporterie was one of them. The *gazogène* bus he was taking to Pau was stopped by a patrol of Germans who were so excited that they'd forgotten to put on their caps or helmets before they roared out of the barracks looking for Maquis. Several of them jumped on the running board of the old bus, waving machine guns, blocking the doorway as they shouted at everyone, "*Raus, raus.*" Get out, get out.

The frightened passengers complied quickly. They were ordered into a control post in the courtyard of the German regional headquarters at Pau. An officer sat at a desk with a phone, rapidly interrogating suspects.

Laporterie showed his identity papers, then was questioned.

"Where are you going?"

"To Pau."

"What for?"

"To see the prefect."

"Aha. If you're going to see the prefect, then you must have an appointment."

"Yes."

"So he is expecting you."

"Yes."

The officer picked up the phone and called the office of the prefect in Pau. Laporterie stood in front of the desk surrounded by justified suspicion. He was not going to see the prefect. He had no appointment. The prefect knew nothing of his predicament.

He looked innocently at the officer. The officer said, "Prefect's office? Yes? Hold on." He passed the receiver to Laporterie and ordered, "Talk." Then he picked up the *écouteur*, the second earpiece of a French phone, to listen in.

Thinking he was talking to the prefect, Laporterie said, "Hello, *Monsieur le préfet*, this is Raoul Laporterie. I'm sorry, I'm going to be late for our meeting."

"That's all right," said the voice of the assistant prefect, Tomasini, who was a good friend of Laporterie's, "I'll wait for you. When can you get here?"

"I don't know — there's a *contrôle*. I'll come as soon as I can."

He hung up. The officer, satisfied that he was probably a minor collaborator because he had friends in the Vichy administration, let him go.

When he got to the office Laporterie discovered from Tomasini that the prefect had been sent to Germany a few days before because he was suspected of Resistance activities. Tomasini was filling in for him. He had guessed Laporterie was in trouble because of the attack on the barracks, followed by the abrupt words of the officer with the German accent.

Laporterie reported to his Resistance colonel, Monnet, that day. The colonel handed him a check, saying, "Cash this please, as quickly as possible. We need the money right away."

Laporterie found a teller whom he knew slightly at the bank, greeted her pleasantly, trying to indicate without saying too much that he was in a hurry, on a "delicate mission," as he liked to say. The teller apparently understood, because she cashed the check right away.

Laporterie took the money to Monnet, who was very pleased to see him back so fast.

"What's going on?" Laporterie asked.

Monnet apologized. One of his colleagues had shot a German officer in the Maquis raid the night before, then searched the body for money and arms. He had stolen the check, which was made out to the dead German. Monnet offered to cash it. Knowing that Laporterie would accept the mission regardless of the danger, Monnet had said nothing to him, figuring that if Laporterie were questioned he would be safer knowing nothing. Monnet had told Laporterie to hurry, because as soon as the Germans realized the body had been robbed, they would lay a trap for the killer.

Sometime in late 1943 or early 1944, Laporterie was informed that a German agent known only as U-25 was tracking him. He was already doing as much as he could to disguise himself, so he kept on working just as he had before.

Hitler's Thousand Year Reich was cracking east, west and overhead, but he went on trying to fortify it. Millions of men were fighting the Russians in the east, more millions were working on the Atlantic "wall" that Hitler hoped would keep out the Allies. If the wall held, his new array of secret weapons, including long-range rockets, jet planes, V-1 missiles, electrosubmarines and the intercontinental bombers being tested at Mont-de-Marsan would give him victory.

The British, Canadians and Americans, who were now planning the decisive assault to crack that wall, needed all the information they could get about the blockhouses, forts and bunkers where the sea-facing guns were. The area near Bordeaux interested Winston Churchill, who insisted that the Allies could land a small force soon after D-day to seize the port, which could then play a crucial role in supplying equipment to Allied armies. Sitting in a conference of chiefs of staff at No. 10 Downing Street about 6 P.M. on February 8, 1944, Churchill said he was "not necessarily wedded to the choice of Bordeaux as the place for the force to land." But he did look to the "low-lying territory" in that part of France.[3] Soon after that, Laporterie was asked by his British contact to get as much information as he could about the coast south of Bordeaux between Spain and Arcachon.

These coastal hills were well fortified because the immense beaches of Landes offered easy access to landing craft. The Germans were preparing for the possibility that the invasion of Europe might come like the invasion of North Africa — direct from North American ports.

Laporterie planned the operation with Vinet in the hotel, probably over many glasses of Noilly. He would have to go by land. But the whole coast was in the forbidden zone, which was extremely difficult and dangerous to enter, except of course for the civilian workers — many of them slave laborers from the east — who were actually building the bunkers for Todt, the giant German construction company. Probably at this point in the discussion, Laporterie and Vinet laughed. Except for the workers — of course. With the right clothes, the right papers, the right attitude — all of which he could provide off the rack — Laporterie could go into the area, right into the forts, as easily as a German. In fact, why not become a German? He already had a German identity card.

Vinet wangled an ambulance for him, perhaps from the base at Pau. Laporterie got papers identifying him as *Bauführer*, or construction chief, working on the construction of the line. He persuaded a young man to volunteer to help him, probably some Maquisard (member of the Resistance) he had helped to evade the STO. He was told not to eat or shave for a couple of days. When he looked properly sick, they dressed him as a Todt worker, smeared some blood on his leg, wrapped it in bandages and loaded him into the ambulance. Laporterie packed two bottles of wine and some lunch, climbed behind the wheel and set off.

He got into the forbidden zone on his pass, saying he was taking the injured worker to hospital. Then he went north, first marking down on paper the immense concrete bunker high on a sand hill that guarded the approaches to the north end of Biarritz. (This bunker was so big and strong that it was too difficult to remove after the war. It remained standing until mid-1986, a bizarre tourist attraction, growing its own dunes with grasses on its flat top.) Laporterie noted as best he could the embrasures hollowed into the stone cliffs near Biarritz, which the soldiers could reach only by swinging down rope ladders.

For almost 200 kilometers, he drove north past Anglet, Boucau, Capbreton, Seignosse, Hossegor, Soustons, Azur, Léon, Lit, Bias, Mimizan-Plage, Biscarosse, to Arcachon, a town built on sandy hills overlooking a huge natural harbor west of Bordeaux.

All along the coast, the half-starved slaves were pouring cement, building roads that would defend them against their liberators. They lived in ugly prison camps spread throughout the region, in Labouheyre, Buglose, Pissos, Daugnague, Sabres, Biscarosse. Some of them were Senegalese — tall black men like those beside whom Laporterie had fought in 1918, now being treated very badly by the Germans. There were also Maquisards and Russian prisoners, who had no hope left. The Russians were especially pitiable, because Stalin regarded them as traitors to be executed if they survived the German camps.

They stopped somewhere near Mimizan-Plage, where Laporterie rapidly sketched a diagram of the beach fortifications for Churchill and friends. After lunch, he made a point of peeing on one of the blockhouses that was temporarily unoccupied. Then they drove on. They completed the trip without trouble, got out of the forbidden zone and went back to Pau, where Laporterie delivered to his British contact a complete diagram of the German fortifications for almost 200 kilometers of Atlantic coast.

After an attack by the Maquis later that spring, this time in Jurançon, a southwestern suburb of Pau, German troops hurried out by truck to catch the Maquisards. As they were returning in the darkness of early morning, the Germans who had been left to garrison Pau thought the incoming trucks were

Maquis. They opened fire. The Germans in the trucks jumped off, hid and returned the fire on their hidden countrymen, assuming the shots came from the Maquis.

Vinet and Laporterie, who guessed what was happening, could see the muzzle flashes and some tracer lines in the valley below them. They laughed. Suddenly Vinet, well aware of the art of Goethe, Beethoven and Schiller to which the men below were heir, said, "There is no such thing as civilization."

About this time, May 12, 1944, the commissioner of police for the third district — the Jewish quarter — of Bordeaux, wrote to his superior officer that "there are no more Jews in the district."[4]

CHAPTER 11

The Burning of Grenade

W HILE EVERYTHING was in doubt after the
Allies landed in Normandy on D-day, June 6, 1944, Maquisards
all over France were wild to fight Germans. Pride demanded
action. To be liberated without fighting was like being conquered without resisting. The Maquisards believed in de
Gaulle's words: "There is no France without a sword in her
hand." But Laporterie, who had risked his life for years for
French pride, saw the consequences of Maquis attacks much
more clearly than the Maquis members did themselves. He saw
disaster.

The German units in the area were still far too strong for the
local Maquis. Near Toulouse was stationed one of the most
powerful armored units in the world, the Panzer division Das
Reich. In Aire-sur-l'Adour, Mont-de-Marsan and Pau were still
many thousands of experienced soldiers equipped with the
latest weapons that the Ruhr factories could make for them. All
the Maquis could do was sting the Germans, who would then,
if they couldn't find the Maquis responsible, react savagely
against civilians.

So Laporterie rebuked the eight or nine boys from Grenade
who had shot up a car full of Germans on the road to Mont-
de-Marsan. The Germans fled and the boys drove back to
Grenade as excited as if they had scored a major victory.

Laporterie told them to stop such nonsense. "Don't you realize the Germans will take reprisals? What if they find you and send you to the camps? Or shoot you right here in front of the church? Quit it."

Laporterie himself was torn when his old friend René Vielle came to him a few days after D-day to ask him to make *brassards*, identifying arm bands for the Forces Françaises de l'Intérieur, who became known as the FFI. Vielle was a burly, loud, strong-willed man determined to fight Germans as soon as possible. Ready to risk his own life, he did not hesitate at the prospect of German reprisals against civilians. Laporterie agreed to make the arm bands. He also offered Vielle the two dozen pistols in his backyard at Bascons, and some meat for the Maquisards.

The red, white and blue arm bands made by Laporterie's seamstresses gave the little guerrilla band military status in their own eyes but none in the Germans'. The arm bands showed that they were Frenchmen openly fighting for France on her own soil, which no one had done since 1940. The words Forces Françaises de l'Intérieur signaled a fateful change in the way Frenchmen thought of themselves. They expressed an idea new in French thought, that France was the interior of something else greater than itself. Before, it had been all by itself, independent of the cosmos. Now, it was inside that cosmos, being consumed.

The Germans were anxious. For years they had walked the streets of France in safety, doing and taking as they liked, because they were the legitimate authority of France through Pétain. Now they had lost that authority because the French, seeing help on the way, found help in themselves. The Germans could rely only on force without respect; all they could expect was resistance animated by hatred. Having conquered France, the Germans now felt besieged in it. Wire mesh went up over the windows of their barracks. They inflicted desperate punishments on innocent hostages for the murder of one of their own, as terrorists do. The south of France, which had been a place of rest for German troops stunned by the blows of the Russians, the British or the North Americans, became a menacing place for soldiers alone on the streets. They could no longer go out alone, or befriend Frenchwomen.

General von Blaskowitz, commanding Army Group G, in southwest France, asked OKW (army headquarters) just after the Allies landed in early June to formally declare the southwest of France a battle zone. His men now lived behind steel-and-stone protection. They traveled by convoy, without the right of tranquil possession, which they thought they had paid for in blood by their deal with Pétain. All this irritated, then baffled and finally enraged the Germans. So the tragedies of Grenade and Oradour-sur-Glane were prepared.

On the night of June 12, Vielle heard from a friend in Aire-sur-l'Adour that the Maquis there had attacked some Germans, who were now fleeing on foot on the highway toward Grenade. Vielle immediately decided to attack these stragglers as they passed.

Perhaps he did not know what had just happened in Oradour-sur-Glane after a similar attack. The Das Reich division from Toulouse had been ordered north to take part in the battle of Normandy. As it neared Oradour-sur-Glane, north of Grenade, it was attacked by Maquis, who wounded or killed some of the Germans. The Germans seized Oradour, machine-gunned or burned about 190 men to death, herded all the women and children, numbering about 500, into the church, then set fire to it, killing them.

Laporterie was not a member of Vielle's unit, but his old friend asked him on the night of June 12 to help round up supplies. Laporterie was wary because he had noticed already that the lights of the post office across the road from La Petite Maison had been on all night so far, always a sign of danger. Yet despite his suspicions that the Germans were aware of Maquis preparations, he delivered some of the FFI arm bands to Vielle during his visit to Vielle's private office in Grenade.

Vielle asked him to get ready bandages, medicines and stretchers for the battle he was anticipating early the next day. At first Vielle was in high spirits: the long wait was over, and at last he and his men could throw themselves into action. But as darkness rose in the quiet valley, and the long shadows fell over them from the wooded hills to the west, Vielle grew moody. They walked over the iron bridge into Larrivière, a small group planning their own liberation, or death. Around midnight, Vielle was somber. He drew Laporterie aside to tell him that he was very much afraid of a disaster the next day, because he now thought his men were losing their will to fight. He sighed and finished, "There's nothing left to do. We'll see."

That same evening, one of Mme Lemée's tenant farmers was warned by a nurse in a hospital nearby that the Germans were planning reprisals along the road to Aire. The farmer warned Lemée, who then sent one of the farm boys to warn the farmers along the road toward Grenade. No warning was given to anyone in Grenade.

Vielle and his nine men walked along the peaceful curving road that runs beside the river out of Larrivière, then crossed again by boat farther up to station themselves at a crossroads by a farm. They waited.

Toward dawn, they heard the Germans walking along talking, their guns at the ready. Vielle gave the order to fire. The lead Germans scattered and returned the fire. The Germans following fled. Lieutenant Walter Schoff fell in the grass by the side of the road, calling out. Vielle, stepping out from behind a tree, was immediately shot and killed. The lights of German motorcycles shone down the road. The French picked up Vielle and ran back toward the river. Vielle was left in a farmhouse, and the rest of the Maquis escaped across the river in the boat. The Germans immediately searched the countryside, finding Vielle's body in the house. Others took Walter Schoff to hospital in Mont-de-Marsan where he soon died.

The German convoy arrived in Grenade in a rage. They

immediately surrounded the *mairie*, sent patrols through the town, set up machine-gun posts commanding the streets and squares, smashed the doors of the school, dragged half-clothed people from their houses, threatened to machine-gun them, looked in their cupboards for Maquisards, bashing anyone who resisted. One young friend of the Laporteries scurried behind a house bordering the river, with a German behind him shouting and shooting. The boy jumped in the river and swam underwater to a landing stage that stuck up high because the river level had recently dropped. He hung there silently until the Germans gave up.

The Germans arrested three suspects, then abruptly left the village.

Laporterie, convinced they would return, feared that they would take hostages, especially men and boys, so he rounded up a dozen of the adolescent boys remaining in the village and led them on foot along the six-kilometer road to Bascons. As they passed the train station half a kilometer from the center of town, a single German soldier with a rifle, who had fled the Vielle attack, walked wearily out of the fields. He asked Laporterie how to get to Mont-de-Marsan. Laporterie pointed him north along the tracks that led across the fields of the Château de Myredé to Mont-de-Marsan. The soldier disappeared down the tracks. Like the Pied Piper, Laporterie led his crowd of boys to Bascons.

Someone in Bascons shouted out the news a little while later — "Fire, fire." From the direction of Grenade rose black smoke. Laporterie started to run toward Grenade, but a friend grabbed his arm and begged him not to go. "Don't go. They'll just kill you, too."

He turned back into town and ran up the narrow winding wooden stairs to the top of the church belfry. He could see black columns of smoke writhing in the air over Grenade. He couldn't stand it. He ran back down the stairs and started for Grenade.

This time the Germans had roared into the town as wild as Maquis boys, firing machine guns. The officer jumped out of his car, firing his pistol around the square where the *mairie* stood. A plane strafed the town from overhead.

Laure and Irène were crouching under a table in the corner of their kitchen to shield themselves from the bullets, when a young man burst into the house and ran upstairs to them. "I've never told you this before," he said, " but I'm in the Resistance, I work for the British. Please hide me."

"Where can I hide you," said Irene. "Not in the house — they'll find you." Laure glanced upward. Irène quickly said, "There's a trapdoor over there, up to the attic."

The boy clambered up. The Germans in the street were firing and shouting "*Raus, raus!*" Irène and Laure went downstairs, out the door, along the narrow main street to the small square in front of the *mairie*, the cannon still firing at the church, the plane strafing the town, the soldiers kicking them and hitting them with the butts of their guns.

Soldiers ran into the school, where the children were about to reenter for their afternoon classes, and set fire to it. The cannon mounted on the half-track vehicle blew in the walls of houses and public buildings. For twenty minutes, they shot up buildings in town as the school went up in flames. Many houses started to burn with people in them; the *mairie*, along with the school and many houses near it, were bombarded. Laure's aunt came weeping along the street, followed by a German soldier carrying a wineskin, repeating, "*Moi pas responsable, moi pas responsable*" (I'm not responsible). He offered her wine, trying to console her.

Most of the people in the square were middle-aged women or children, with a sprinkling of boys and old men, because most of the men had fled, or were in a prison camp in Germany, or in a labor camp somewhere in Hitler's Europe. Many of the people were wounded by the cannon fire, and at least four of the men were beaten up. Into the square the

Germans herded the whole population, weeping, ashamed, frightened, defiant.

A sergeant standing in front of one of the burning houses beside the woman who had lived in it pulled out a bottle of schnapps, took a swig and handed it to her saying sadly, "*Mauvaise guerre . . . guerre nicht gut.*"

Speaking German from the steps of the *mairie*, the German officer demanded through an interpreter to know the names of the terrorists. If they were not given up, worse would follow. People in the crowd protested. The German threatened, yelled, but no one denounced Vielle and his men. The officer waited. Still no one spoke.

"All right, all the men from seventeen to twenty-three against the wall."

A few young men walked to the wall.

"Not enough," said the German.

"The others have gone to work in Germany," said Mayor Brousse. "Or they're working in the fields. This is an agricultural community."

"There are terrorists in Grenade," said the German. "A German soldier has been killed. If anything like that ever happens again, this whole village will be burned to the ground and the people deported."

The Germans then inspected the papers of all the men between twenty-three and sixty. They took thirty hostages, nearly all young men, put them into their trucks and roared out of Grenade toward Mont-de-Marsan.

As Laporterie emerged onto the sunny road from the woods that border Bascons to the southwest, a German plane flew over. It dipped toward him, and he clambered over the high bank edging the road and hid in the hedgerow. He heard it firing. The plane disappeared toward Grenade. He jumped down from the hedgerow and kept on walking with a wary eye on the sky.

He found the people of Grenade stunned by the violence.

Nothing like this had occurred in the region since medieval times, when the British general Montgomery had terrorized the countryside in a campaign for Aquitaine. Most of the houses in the north end of the village were destroyed, along with the school and the police station. The houses burned for days. The single fire engine broke down repeatedly. Women with tears of grief or smoke in their eyes searched the hot wreckage for whatever they could salvage; others went to Mont-de-Marsan or even Bordeaux to beg for the lives of their men.

In the middle of suffering there was a moment of happiness for Laure, Raoul and Irène, who were reunited safely. They took in Laure's Aunt Marie-Louise Proëres, and her daughter Colette, whose house had been destroyed. But the reunion was brief, for the Germans soon came back to garrison the town. Laporterie had to run again.

Within a week, the Germans in Mont-de-Marsan released eight of the Grenade hostages, then another four from Bordeaux. The remaining eighteen were ordered on to the second-to-last train to leave Bordeaux for Dachau.

Laporterie received, on July 10, a letter in code from Irène.

My dear sir:

A few words from our little corner of the world. We're all fine and I hope it's the same with you. The weather is still bad, which is not good for our morale. But the good weather will surely come, so we wait patiently hoping it won't be long.

Business has been good but we are lacking certain perfumes. We are missing Yalomiel for the hands and Cucumber Milk. The perfumers aren't attending to business just now, but it is advisable despite everything not to make any changes. So wait patiently a little longer, that's what one of the salesmen advises. Everything is fine here. I embrace you very affectionately.

Kiki

The translation from Kiki's code, which she had arranged with her father just before he left, runs like this:

> The Germans (perfumers) are still here (weather is bad) but they are leaving (perfume is missing); already two units (Yalomiel and Cucumber Milk) have gone. They're not bothering us much, but the Maquis say you shouldn't come home yet.

The Maquis was never as aggressive as now, when the Allied successes in the north made liberation certain. But the Germans had never done as much harm in the area as at that moment, when punishment was pointless and vengeance soon avenged. In Portet, to the southwest, in late June, during a Maquis attack, dozens of Germans and Maquis died when a village was burned; in Estang, near Mont-de-Marsan, in Barcelonne, Aire, Mont-de-Marsan itself, Geaune and many other rural communities, crossroads hamlets or towns, Frenchmen and Germans who came from similar little places patriotically killed one another.

In the same week that the Canadian and American armies were closing the trap on a quarter of a million desperately struggling Germans encircled in the Falaise-Argentan pocket, the Germans under von Blaskowitz were sending soldiers into French villages to murder civilians for breaking "racial laws." A German detachment surrounded Le Houga, and soldiers burst into the hotel run by Mlle Lafontan.

"Who have you got here?" demanded the officer.

"Boarders," said Lafontan. The German slapped her hard in the face.

As Lafontan held off the Germans, three Jews whom she had been sheltering, M. and Mme Khom and M. Stoppler, tried to escape through the garage door, but were caught. The Germans seized three suspected Maquisards, shot them, arrested Lafontan along with the Jews and four others, put a bomb under the hotel, blew it up and drove away.

CHAPTER **12**

A Night of Liberty, a Dawn of Sorrow

NOW THINGS HAPPENED that were as im-
probable as legend. Men in suits swung by their necks from
lampposts all along the main street of Tulle. A French army
invaded France over the beaches of the Côte d'Azur. Five
hundred mothers and babies were deliberately burned alive in
a church. Soldiers from Quebec landed by parachute to liberate
French villages their ancestors had left 300 years before. All the
huge Condor bombers rose off the runways, never to return.

Laporterie was in paradoxical danger during the last few
weeks of the German occupation of the south precisely because
the Vichy government, which had been oppressing him, was
collapsing. The Germans, no longer trusting Vichy, nevertheless couldn't rule in open conflict with their only allies in
France. So they let Vichy officials, a group to whom Laporterie
still nominally belonged, run the minor civil affairs, while they
pursued resisters, as well as their usual target minorities. The
courageous Vichy officials who openly resisted or protested
were punished. For clandestine resistance, the Germans retali-
ated by imprisoning or deporting other Vichy officials. Mass
resignations of course ensued. France, while it was being liberated, slid toward chaos, as de Gaulle had feared. The collabo-

rators now grew almost as savage as the Germans in their determination to hurt the Resistance as much as they could. In effect the collaborators were taking revenge for the revenge that was sure to come, provoking hatred so intense that for some people it was like civil war.[1]

Mayor Larrieu argued desperately with Colonel Bauer, commander of the retreating Germans, not to annihilate Mont-de-Marsan. "The people will think badly of Germany," he said. "And think of your own personal reputation." The Germans spared the city, some of them heading south toward refuge in Spain, others northeast toward Germany. Von Blaskowitz, seeing the French army and the Americans rolling up his line of retreat toward Lyon, while the Allies hammered the Wehrmacht in Normandy, began to withdraw. Some of the Germans who had already left Mont-de-Marsan were sent back to seize the air base again. At Pont-de-Bats, near Mont-de-Marsan, in late August, the British Captain T. A. Mellows, leading a group of Allied and Maquisard soldiers despite a wounded knee, was killed in the final battle to liberate the city. Some of the defeated Germans drove north to fight again. Others, carrying paintings, gold, jewelry, whatever loot they could pick up, fled over the border into Spain. These, the first German refugees since the exodus of the Jews and anti-Hitler resisters, were the first of many thousands who abandoned Hitler and Nazi Germany in the approaching year of devastation. They were living at ease in Spain while Germany went up in flames.

After the battle of Pont-de-Bats, they knew they were free. General Leclerc was marching on Paris along with the mighty United States Army, Frenchmen were speeding up the Rhône toward Lyon, the British and Canadians were liberating northern France. Von Blaskowitz had fled, leaving a nightmare memory so strong that people obeyed the habits of fear of him and everything German long after they were free.

Mont-de-Marsan, Grenade and Bascons were *en fête*. The

brass bands marched in the streets, the people danced and drank and kissed and left their lights shining at night. Laporterie had a joyful reunion with Friquet and the manager, Mme Hortense, in the store. He drank toasts to the victorious Allies in the Café de la Poste where he had years before written out his reports with Friquet in front of the Germans, and plotted with Tachon to resurrect the dead for his passengers. The hospitable Landais had been deprived of the joy of seeing one another for so long that weddings and other festivities became more or less public affairs, where anyone could turn up, uninvited but sure of a welcome. It took years for the Landais to make up the loss of one another's society.

De Gaulle marched into Paris, across the great square in front of the cathedral of Notre-Dame-de-Paris chanting the "Te Deum" while snipers' bullets sang off the stones. As soon as he had consolidated his hold on the capital through the army and the police, he headed for the southwest, to Toulouse, "a city considerably disturbed."[2] Many factions contended: Russian Vlassovites, Spaniards, Gaullists, communists, Maquis, FFI. Laporterie cheered de Gaulle marching through the streets here and in Bordeaux, supported him at official receptions and sent off a telegram of support to the general in Paris, assuring him of the loyalty of the people of Bascons. Such telegrams were prized by de Gaulle, who needed to prove not only to the fractious French politicians but also to the British and Americans that he was the only possible government of the moment.

Soon after the liberation of Landes in August 1944, Laporterie's old friend Colonel Weill came to Grenade with a letter and a gun. After they embraced, Weill gave Laporterie the letter, in which he described some of what Laporterie had done during the long German occupation of France:

From the beginning, Laporterie has been the most devoted of our distributors of *Franc Tireur* in Landes. From June 1940 on, Laporterie, acting as a French citizen, never accepted the armistice. Out of simple kindness, he passed many patriots over the demarcation line. He hid, with the greatest altruism, Frenchmen of the Israelite faith. I can attest from the most reliable sources, that M. Laporterie was the object of the most alluring offers and that he never accepted any pay at all for these services. I consider it a duty to state that he is a true French patriot.

"Now, I'm looking for that son of a bitch Chebassier," said Weill. "Do you know where I can find him?"

"What for?" said Laporterie. He was stalling to find out what Weill was planning to do.

"I've got a present for him," Weill said, patting the bulge in his jacket pocket.

Laporterie was appalled. "Listen, you've got the wrong man."

"Wasn't he running the hotel then? I know it was the guy running the hotel."

"Yes, but he didn't denounce you."

They argued. Laporterie was certain Chebassier was innocent. Weill believed he wasn't. Secretly, Laporterie sent his nephew Pierrot across the street to warn Chebassier, who fled. Months later, Weill thanked Laporterie for stopping him. He now believed Chebassier was not the culprit, although he was never able to find out who it was.

Weill's letter and many others like it were not only a satisfaction to Laporterie, but a protection, because like many clandestine Resistance members, he was suspected by some people of having collaborated. The communists particularly disliked him, perhaps because they saw in his family background the conditions that according to Leninists produce the agricultural proletariat or peasantry that inevitably must wage war against the landowners and aristocrats. Yet Laporterie's whole career had disproved the theory of the inevitability of class warfare. He had also demonstrated, without ever working out any theory, that it was possible to peacefully maintain civilized values in the face of the most violent tyranny in Europe. In the fall of 1944, he received a threatening anonymous letter denouncing him as a plutocrat and threatening vengeance against him from the left. The police checked the typewriters of various suspects, but the culprit was never found.

Laporterie, like France, was deeply divided after the liberation. He was at first amazed and amused by the antics of the do-nothings who joined the Resistance after the Germans had left. But like Tachon, he was disgusted by these antics, especially when he realized that some people were actually getting away with it. These were the collaborators — for whom Bordeaux was famous — who learned to "waltz without turning their heads," in the famous phrase of Gabriel Delaunay, the regional delegate for Bordeaux of de Gaulle's Rassemblement des Résistants pour la Reconstruction et la Renovation de la France.

In a speech to the war veterans' association of Grenade, including the society of ex-prisoners of war, which he had been president of, Laporterie vehemently denounced the collaborators. The full rigor of the law should be applied to them, he said. No mercy should be shown to these traitors who damaged France while others were fighting for her. But in fact he was making a thinly disguised plea not for vengeance but for forgiveness. He sidled up to his purpose this way because he believed in disguising the unpalatable. "The truth will be accepted if it is just a bit disguised." In this case, he satisfied the passions of his audience for vengeance, while he was actually leading them to more temperate views. As a senior member of the Liberation Committee of Grenade, he wrote and presented to the *préfecture* at Mont-de-Marsan a toughly worded motion on behalf of the committee, stating eloquently the feelings of many true resisters represented by the committee:

> I have suffered too much from the enemy occupation of
> our country and from the tyrannous regime of the usurpers

in the so-called government of Vichy, not only in my business but also in my dearest affections, as in the beliefs I profess in human justice and liberty, not to demand with all my power the most pitiless punishment for all those great or small who became accomplices of the enemy and leaders of the political collaboration; but to comply with flagrant judicial mistakes, even if they are exceptional, or to condemn on appearances or presumptions alone, would be to my eyes to violate our ideal of justice and our thirst for fair play.

To do that would in addition gravely weaken the judgments against the truly guilty . . . and prevent us from returning to the healthy republican traditions that have made us great.

He then demanded that the files concerning the accused be opened at once to his committee. If this weren't done right away, all the members of the committee would resign en masse.

So Laporterie had to lead his fellow resisters in the defense of the ideals of civilization against their fellow citizens. Not all the enemies of France had left with the Germans.

The rhetoric worked, for the easygoing Landais cannot carry the burden of vengeance very far. When, in his office in Bascons a few weeks later, Laporterie was actually confronted with a weeping woman seeking his protection from villagers who were denouncing her, he took pity on her. They wanted to shave her bald, then parade her through the streets half-naked in rags because she had been too close to the Germans, they said. Her crime was worse because her husband had been a prisoner in Germany the whole time she had consorted with his enemies. Laporterie knew there was truth in the charges, but he also saw what they were overlooking: the woman had been on the edge of starvation most of the time because her husband had been unable to help her.

He hid her in the *mairie* while he went out to talk to the

people. He managed to persuade them that although she was guilty she should be forgiven.

A man he knew slightly, Grimand in the *préfecture* at Pau, was also among the accused. Laporterie supported Grimand, who expressed the anguish of the accused collaborators in a letter poignantly reminiscent of the Jewish refugees:

> Thank you, dear sir, once again for your loyal support. Your good wishes are even more necessary now than before. I'm living in anguish these days. Who has paid for whom? Where will this horror stop?

In early September 1944, he received a letter by hand from Lestelle-Betharram dated September 1. The letter read:

> Dear M. Raoul:
> I hope you and your family are in good health. Because the mail isn't working properly, we don't know what's happening. Also, I can't phone or telegraph you.
> At last we are free, our joy reduced by the absence of our old people. Maybe Heaven will grant us the miracle of returning them in good health.
> I will leave for Bordeaux as soon as there is a train or a bus. I hope to find a furnished apartment so we can settle down before school, and get back to the store, etc.
> In the hope of hearing good news from you, I take you by the hand with gratitude.
> > Your very appreciative friend

The letter was signed Grenier, although the Germans had been gone for weeks.

Freedom for the Yaeches in their mountain village was first the absence of fear. The Germans, from one day to the next, were gone, almost without a trace. The Yaeches hurried down to Bordeaux as soon as it was safe to look for traces of Sarah's parents. There was nothing. They had been gone for more than a year, and there was never any word from them again.

Yaeche retrieved his store, then eventually the apartment, but the kind of life they had led before was irretrievable. Friends and relatives were missing, presumed gassed, others came back from hiding with bizarre stories and psychological wounds that might never heal. Yaeche immediately wrote to Laporterie to thank him. Even though he was busy trying to rebuild a life for himself and his children and Sarah, he took time to make sure that Laporterie had all the recognition in Bordeaux he needed and deserved. When he heard of Laporterie's financial troubles at La Petite Maison, he rounded up money for Laporterie among the surviving Jews; he sent a young clerk trained in the business to help manage the main store in Mont-de-Marsan; he wrote letters to the papers, to the Grand Rabbi of Bordeaux, to various people in government, describing what Laporterie had done.

Yaeche became a leader of the Jews of Bordeaux in the honoring of Laporterie, so much so that when Sarah and he heard of the trouble between the Angel family, whom Laporterie had crossed, and Mme Laure Laporterie, they immediately took the side of Mme Laure. The Angels, completely forgetting what the Laporteries had done for them and the fears they had and the death the Laporteries had averted for them, were accusing Laure of stealing the coat Mme Angel had given her in 1941. Sarah Yaeche could not contain her fury at what she believed was the ingratitude and the greed of the Angels. When she heard that Laure was returning the coat, Sarah offered to go to Grenade to get the coat for Mme Angel. Once she had it in her hands, she slashed off all the fur and shoved the denuded skin at Mme Angel.

Yaeche urged his fellow citizens, Jews and Christians, to recognize what Laporterie had done. He did not make much headway because in the official myth now rapidly forming about the events of 1940 to 1944, there was little place for the saviors in Bascons and Le Chambon. In a paroxysm of guilt, rage and lies, French officialdom tried to shift the blame for its failures as far as possible from themselves. About ten to twelve thousand collaborators were executed by kangaroo courts soon after the liberation. This was called the purification. The collaborationist sympathies of hundreds of thousands of people, perhaps a million or two, were supposed to have been expunged by the murder of ten to twelve thousand scapegoats.

What people wanted to believe they set about symbolizing, like religious idols. Myth after myth was sculpted to fit the empty niches in the French pantheon: the Germans were responsible for the war, the French army was outnumbered in 1940; the Germans had more and better equipment; the Resistance of 1944 was in embryo in 1940, a Resistance army of fighters such as Jean Moulin had fought side by side with the Allies as equals to liberate the country, which resulted, de Gaulle said, in the "miracle of our victory";[3] the collaborators were few, without great importance; France was needed in her colonies to carry out her civilizing mission. The myth that contained all the others was that France was a great power.

To demonstrate all these things, stories were told, people murdered, books written, truths suppressed, documents destroyed and new wars begun. In 1945, de Gaulle begged money and arms from the Americans for an expeditionary force to Indochina to drive out Ho Chi Minh's communists. So at the end of one disaster, de Gaulle prepared another for his country. France under de Gaulle was like a bum waking up from a drunk to stagger along looking for the same old poison: greedy factionalism (called politics); colonial wars (called the civilizing mission of France); the vicious maltreatment of helpless opponents — Algerians, Germans, Vietnamese — (called the greatness of French arms). All of this was thought to lead to the mythical place called the Glory of France.

The dust of forgetting was already settling over the cowardly fascism of France in the 1930s, the collaborationists, the anti-Semitism of Vichy, and the heroism of hundreds of thousands of French families, usually in villages, who risked their lives, their comfort and food, to save the lives of Jews. Of the approximately 330,000 Jews in France in 1940, about 250,000 were saved. Probably all of them were helped at some point by French Christians who risked the death camps in order to help their fellow citizens. Because each family was usually lodged or fed by a French family at some point and received illegal papers from officials, it is quite possible that for every Jew saved, one to four French people risked death. Thus, somewhere between 250,000 and 1,000,000 French people risked their lives to help the strangers at the gate. In no other country in Europe were so many Jews saved; in no other country did so many risk so much for their neighbors. In no other country was there such blind forgetting of the good things people do.

The flag of the fifty-second Mitrailleurs of Indochina flew in the sun of the Midi over Raoul Laporterie's head at a ceremony in Bascons in early 1945, honoring the *mort pour la patrie* of the region, while encouraging others to die for France in Indochina. Present at the ceremony, nominally to open a new court for the game of *fronton*, was a delegation of the Sephardim of Bordeaux who had been saved by Laporterie. Laporterie and Yaeche stood with tears of pride in their eyes, and of affection for each other, as the flag that symbolized the oppression of Vietnam was honored with salutes in their newly liberated country. Laporterie expressed the mythologizing of France under de Gaulle succinctly in his speech, saying:

> If the flag recalls dark days, it also signifies that although its soldiers were temporarily off the battlefield through the chance of war, France herself had never ceased to look

upon them as true soldiers who lost none of our admiration despite being held hostage.

Calling the cloth on the pole above him "glorious" he went on:

> This standard expresses my pride at finding myself among such men, my desire that their patriotic actions as soldiers without uniform in the clandestine struggle for the liberation of their country be remembered, my hope that their heroism will always be commemorated by generations to come, who will keep close to their hearts the need for reunions such as this as often as possible to continue the noble traditions of the Resistance and the Maquis, which are expressed in two noble words, Fatherland and Freedom.

No one had a better right to say it; no Allied country was less worthy to hear it. As he spoke, trainloads of German prisoners rolled through Mont-de-Marsan on their way to starvation in the death camps of Landes.

CHAPTER **13**

The French and
American Death Camps

TWO STARVING GERMAN prisoners of war dressed in rags stood at attention in front of Raoul Laporterie in the prison camp at Mont-de-Marsan. Hans Goertz and Adam Heyl had been ordered to report for work in La Petite Maison because they were both experienced tailors, but the wasted men whom Laporterie saw trembling before him were worse than he himself had been in his camp in Germany. The vengeance of the French army had begun.

The rings of exhaustion reminded him of his own imprisonment. His days and nights in the train, in the camps, sickened him again as he questioned the two Germans briefly.

Their hopes were painfully obvious to him: Please get us out of here, we are dying.

"You will come to work for me not as prisoners, but as free men," he said. "Come on, I'll give you some new clothes." At that moment Hans Goertz thought, We're saved.

Unknown to Laporterie and most of the civilians in Landes, the French army was taking vengeance on the Germans by starving them to death. The camp at Buglose, where Goertz had almost died, was one of 1600 camps spread across France and Occupied Germany. Twenty-five percent of the prisoners at Buglose had died in January 1946 of starvation or dysentery.[1]

Goertz, a private in the 329th Infantry, had begun his
captivity in one of the American camps on the banks of the
Rhine river in April 1945. The Americans called these camps
cages because they were simply farmers' fields fenced with
barbed wire. There were no buildings, no roofs, no kitchen, no
hospital. In these corrals, millions of people, including some
women and children, dug holes in the ground for shelter,
received no food — or less than ten percent of a U.S. soldier's
rations — and had little or no water to drink. Within weeks
they were dying like flies. One of the camps was described by
two U.S. Army doctors:

> Rain, snow and bone-chilling wind swept down the valley
> from the north over the flats where the inclosure [sic] was
> located. Huddled close together for warmth, behind the
> barbed wire, was a most awesome sight — nearly 100,000
> haggard, apathetic, dirty, gaunt, blank-staring men clad
> in dirty field gray uniforms, and standing ankle-deep in
> mud. Here and there were dirty white blurs which upon
> a closer look were seen to be men with bandaged heads
> or arms or standing in shirt sleeves! The German com-
> mander reported that the men had not eaten for at least
> two days, and the provision of water was a major prob-
> lem — yet only 200 yards away was the river Rhine
> running bank-full.[2]

Goertz had been captured by the Americans, whom they called
the Amis, on April 2. At first, he was relieved to be captured.
He had kept on fighting through 1945 because if he had
deserted, his mother and father would have been shot by order
of Field Marshal Model, who commanded the German army in
the west. The last letter he had received from his father was
now making a warm patch against his left chest.

All the prisoners in the big American camps at Rheinberg,
Buderich, Remagen, Bad Kreuznach were starving. They were

all living in holes in the ground. They had no medicine. The latrines were logs shoved across ditches. Some of the prisoners were so weak that they fell off the logs and drowned. Their bodies were left there. At Rheinberg, near where Goertz was captured, the prisoners were soon dying at the rate of about 6000 a month.[3] When a man died, a voice announced over the PA system that he had been discharged.

Goertz, a cheerful, obliging young man when he entered the army, had developed a stoical self-reliance during the years of hard fighting he endured in Russia. He learned to ward off sorrow and self-pity in the first few weeks of his captivity. Yes, of course you're very sad, he thought. Who is happy about being captured? He vowed that he would survive the camps as he had survived the fighting around Leningrad when the temperature fell to -50° F. His fingers, feet and even his back were frostbitten, he had been wounded and had lost a finger. He might have despaired, like some of the men, because his hands were so important in his profession — tailoring — but he refused to give in.

Survival depends on hope. Goertz, twenty-four years old, hoped to be repatriated soon, to return to his mother and father in their house north of the Ruhr. At the end of the war in May, the prisoners hoped to begin receiving mail from home, but it was forbidden. Lacking news, the men lived on rumors. The Americans had sold them for a dollar each to the French, who were going to use them as slaves in France. The rumor was credible because the Germans after 1940 had kept one and a half million French prisoners working for years in Germany. It was true that many prisoners were now being transferred to the French, as they could see when the brown trucks bearing the star of the U.S. Army drew up outside the gate. They were there now, their engines idling, as men were called forward by their German officers. Goertz heard his name, got up and started for the gate, holding on to his hope.

He was herded onto one of the trucks, which had been sent

there by command of Colonel Philip S. Lauben of the Supreme Headquarters, Allied Expeditionary Forces (SHAEF) who was chief of the German Affairs Branch of SHAEF. The tailgates slammed shut on the crowd standing within, the drivers accelerated slowly, then braked hard, slamming the tired men forward into a denser pack. More prisoners were shoved in, the tailgates closed and the trucks drove away.

They arrived by train at Rennes in Brittany, where they were marched along a road exposed to the French civilians. At first the civilians who lined up along the way threw stones at them, shouting threats. Several times the American guards fired shots over the crowd to keep them back. They gradually grew quiet when, as one of Goertz's fellow prisoners said, "they realized what terrible shape we were in."[4] Goertz stayed on at the camp at Rennes while his fate was argued out between the French government under de Gaulle and the American army under General Eisenhower.

The French wanted 1.75 million prisoners to help rebuild the country, but they had taken fewer than 300,000 themselves. The Americans agreed to supply more than a million, but when the turnovers began in July 1945, the French were appalled to find that most of the men they were getting were half dead. "We looked like nails," said one of Goertz's fellow prisoners, Heinz T.,[5] who was now so thin that he could knock himself unconscious by moving his arm rapidly once to the side.[6]

Jean-Pierre Pradervand, head of the International Red Cross delegation in France, visited several of the satellite camps around Rennes in August 1945, probably including the camp where Goertz was being held. Pradervand was so worried by the sight of the emaciated men that he tried to telephone Charles de Gaulle, who brushed him off. Pradervand then wrote a long letter to *"mon général,"* offering medicine, clothing and food (some of it supplied by German prisoners in North America).[7] He predicted that because of the atrocious conditions he'd seen in the camps, 200,000 of the 600,000 prisoners in France would certainly die "unless something is done" to improve their conditions before winter. He asked for gasoline so that the Red Cross trucks could take supplies to the camps. In the margin of Pradervand's letter, appears the note *"C'est fait"* (It is done). But nothing was done.

Many of the officers in the camps themselves were outraged by the conditions imposed on them and the prisoners in their care. A few protested vigorously, like Captain Julien of the Third Algerian Rifles, and one of his fellow officers, Lieutenant Soubeiray, who wrote a dangerous letter in his own handwriting damning "the intolerable inhumanity of the regular army."[8] He sent this to his commanding officer. More officers resigned in humiliation and despair, condemning the army for outrages rivaling the Nazi atrocities.[9] Some of the French soldiers shot Germans in their holes at night, some drove over them in jeeps, some refused to allow German civilians to bring food to the men, and one shot a German woman for attempting to feed the starving through the slats of a cattle car. Near Marseille, some French soldiers tormented the prisoners by spilling on the ground water that the thirsty men needed. The men of the 108th Infantry Regiment were so brutal to the prisoners that Lieutenant Colonel de Champvallier, with the knowledge and consent of his commanding officer, General Billotte, asked that the regiment be dissolved.[10]

Pradervand would not give up. He wangled an interview with Eisenhower's chief of staff, General Bedell Smith, in Frankfurt, where he laid photographs of the famished prisoners on Smith's desk. Smith, alarmed, immediately took the photographs in to Eisenhower's office. He then promised to issue extra food for the prisoners. The big Paris paper *Le Figaro* printed several stories that were ineffective in raising public concern because the French army would not give out the shocking death totals or allow the reporter to inspect the camps himself.[11] But *Le Figaro*, now helped by *Le Monde*, frightened Eisenhower into issuing a memo loaded with lies for his staff to use against the press reports.[12] The American ambassador also sent a secret cablegram to the State Department advising it to avoid a confrontation with the French on the issue because there was truth in the French allegations of the American atrocities.[13] And so the story disappeared from the press outside Germany for forty-four years.

In one of the French camps visited by Pradervand, at the village of Thorée-les-Pins, the men predicted by Pradervand to die in winter were already dying. The army quickly filled the first cemetery, then negotiated to buy land for a much bigger one. In the village, the camp was known as Buchenwald. One of the village women who had seen the men in the camp wept when she described them to her friends. Every time she thought of the men thereafter, tears came to her eyes. Soon she refused to talk about it. Others in the village said that the new graveyard was not big enough; the bodies were being taken away by train at night to be disposed of somehow at the big army base near Le Mans.[14]

When Hans Goertz was herded with others into a cattle car he had none of the food or clothing that Eisenhower told the press all prisoners routinely received. Conditions on these French trains were so bad that the officers were under standing orders not to stop the train in stations where the public might see the prisoners. They were packed into cattle cars roofed with a few slats covered with barbed wire. A typical car carried forty men, two small cartons of food, enough for one skimpy meal to last them for two or three or perhaps four days. The toilet was a bucket in the corner. Dying, they rolled slowly south past countryside they had so lately ruled. Through the high hilly Charente, through Bordeaux, into the flat plain of Landes almost to Grenade they went. They arrived at Buglose near St-Paul-les-Dax in the rain. Scarcely able to walk, Goertz shambled along the narrow road while the amazed villagers stared. Prisoners fell down dead in front of them. For more than two kilometers they staggered to a barracks in the pine woods recently occupied by slave laborers building the Atlantic wall.

In those days, when Germany had ruled, the scene had been reversed. Then, Germans had herded French army prisoners from the same station along the same road to the same camp. When they fell, the Germans shot them.

The adjutant of the camp, Maura, told a villager later on that eighty-seven out of the thousand or so men on the train died on that march through the rain and the day after. Their bodies were dumped into a grave or graves without a marker.[15]

Goertz looked around the dirty cabin, furnished with bare wood bunks, under a leaking roof, lit by scummy windows looking out onto a dripping wet pine woods. It was easy to think, This is the place where I die.

Yet the French had told them a pleasant story, perhaps believing it themselves. The prisoners were to work here in the south of France picking grapes and making wine. Goertz imagined himself shoulder-high among the vines in a sunny vineyard, plucking fresh sweet juicy grapes, filling his mouth with them as he filled a cart. The Frenchwomen who would work with him would be kind. They would smile, teaching him French.

The time of the grape harvest arrived. The sun shone, but the prisoners were not sent to help. The French literally had no use for them. They continued to starve. The autumn rains began. Their clothing was, in the word of a French army report, "catastrophic."[16] Goertz had been a tailor before the war, so now when he got the chance at a needle and thread, he painfully stitched up his rags. Always eager to oblige, he sewed up the catastrophic clothes of the others as best he could.

Some of the men were almost naked as winter came on. Their clothing reminded them at every moment of their fate. They could not be seen in public in their indecent rags; therefore, the French did not intend to make them work. Therefore, they were worthless. Their only purpose was to die.

Fritz Foerster, aged forty-nine, shrunk in half by starvation, died on September 13 before the picking began. On October 5, as the picking reached full swing in the country southeast of the camp, Private John Wanzek, aged fifty-five, and Private George Schwanitz, aged seventeen, died.[17] By the end of the season, more than 200 of the men who had marched in the rain were dead. No record was kept at the village *mairie*, although French law requires all deaths to be recorded.

No mail came or went. For many months as he was dragged around France, Goertz had no idea whether his mother and father had been shot or had survived the Allied bombing and invasion. Nor did they have any news of their son. He slept shivering in his rags on wood boards in a bunk infested with lice. The bunks were so infested that when the prisoners forced themselves to drag them outside to tap them on the ground, the lice fell out in a thick rectangle that matched the outline of the bunk.

In the autumn came a priest from the church of St-Vincent-de-Paul at nearby Dax, where Laporterie's boyhood idol had been born. Le Chanoine Jean-Baptiste St-Germain, a thin agonized man, liked to visit the camp in his long black soutane, graciously comforting the suffering.[18] He gave them a sack of apples, he brought five kilos of honey, he buried the Catholics, three to five a day. But the solution to their problem was not in a sack of apples. It was in the minds of the French, which might have been changed, and were not.

The priest comforted the prisoners, but he did not cry out against their suffering. On the wall of his study hung the portrait of the pope he revered, Pius XII, who had never said a word against Hitler's murders of Jews, communists and Gypsies. What St Vincent de Paul had taught was completely forgotten in the church built to honor his memory.

But not in Grenade. Raoul Laporterie knew that some officers in the army who were supposed to be organizing food supplies for the prisoners and for the big cities were in fact selling the desperately needed food on the black market. The profits they kept for themselves, while the farmers were robbed, the prisoners starved and poor people in the cities went short. Angrily he wrote to de Gaulle's government in Paris, heedless of the risk of retaliation.

The French army amazes and disappoints the farmers, who see that the requisitions levied on them don't relieve the painful situation in the cities. The explanation for this is the fact that the military administration which takes for its so-called needs a large part of the requisitions, greatly exaggerates the amount of supplies required, and it seems from all the evidence that all the army's surplus ends up in the black market.[19]

Many of the French who came in direct contact with the prisoners, like the *chanoine* and the villagers around Thorée-les-Pins, Labouheyre and Buglose, acted kindly toward them, apparently never believing that there was any use in appealing to their fellow citizens to end the catastrophe. That the deaths might easily have been averted by an appeal to public opinion is proven by the experience of the prisoners taken by the British and Canadians. Of the approximately three million prisoners held by the British and Canadians in early June 1945,[20] probably fewer than a thousand starved to death. The Red Cross reports of their few visits to these camps rarely register complaints. The health of the prisoners was generally satisfactory, because of the policies of the two armies, which were supported by public opinion.[21]

Among the 5,224,310 prisoners taken by the Americans, about 790,000 died mainly from exposure, unsanitary conditions and starvation.[22] In the French camps holding an average of about 650,000 prisoners for almost two years, then several hundred thousand for two more years, somewhere between 167,000 and 350,000 died in the kind of conditions that killed off twenty-five percent of Goertz's fellow inmates at Labouheyre in January 1946.[23]

The French army regularly received reports of the starvation, death, despair and maltreatment in the camps, always promising to make improvements, and doing virtually nothing. So ragged were these men that the Red Cross inspectors gave them the clothes off their backs and left in their underwear.[24]

The death rate in the German army went up sharply as soon as the war ended, remaining far above wartime levels for many months. The French army put to death far more German prisoners than they killed on the field of battle. More than ten times as many German soldiers died in peacetime in the French and American camps as died in the years of war on the western front from June 1941 to April 1945.

The Americans who, in October 1945, had loudly announced suspension of shipments of their starving prisoners to the French because the French were starving them, quietly resumed their shipments in November. This meant that somewhere between 100,000 and 300,000 more men were delivered to the French camps, while the world supposed that hundreds of thousands were en route home to be restored to health with the help of the U.S. Army. This sort of sleight of hand was illustrated in miniature in Buglose. After a speedy visit from some kind of inspection group known to the villagers as an "Inter-Allied team," most of the ragged survivors were trucked away. Buglose was converted into a "hospital" under Commander J. M. Bernadet, who says to this day that although the camp was "not well organized" before he arrived, conditions immediately improved under the new policy.[25] Deaths, he says, were minimal, only eight or ten in more than a year, all properly recorded in the *mairie* at Mont-de-Marsan. Yet not a single death of a German is recorded for the same period.

Goertz and the rest of the bony evidence were trucked away

to a frightful barracks in the pine woods called Labouheyre, where the dysentery was so bad that even the French guards got it. The men were so weak by now that they had to string ropes from the bunks to the doors so that they could haul themselves out. Goertz, down to fifty-two kilos (115 pounds) from his healthy weight of about ninety-four (207), had to go to the woods every day to chop and saw. The guards, recruited mainly from local farms, took pity on the prisoners. At Buglose, Raphael Conqueré, a villager who worked in the kitchen, brought half a liter of milk every day for three of the prisoners.[26] They said later that they survived only because of this milk. To any prisoner who showed a desire to escape, the guards at Labouheyre turned their backs. Escape to Germany was virtually impossible because the Germans were in rags, penniless, without papers, unable to speak French, yet some of them tried. One of these was discovered a year later, with a long white beard, flitting like a ghost through the woods of Landes. He had survived like an animal for a year while hundreds of others in the camp had died. Then he had the chance to lodge with a local farm family, where he knew he would be well treated; he went into the "free worker" status.

Some 600 survivors of Buglose joined several hundred other prisoners at Labouheyre, where 215 died in the first few months.[27] In the same period in the village of Labouheyre itself, which then numbered about 1900 people, eighteen deaths of French civilians were duly recorded.[28] In proportion, about twenty Germans died for every French civilian.

Goertz was told that he would have to go to work in the mines near Toulouse. He said, "No, I won't stay in France underground," because he had "stayed in the war" to protect his parents, had served a long time on the Russian front, had been wounded three times and was not fit for it. He stayed as a free worker along with his friend, Adam Heyl.

Raoul Laporterie was informed that he was eligible to apply for free workers, who would be paid by the French government while they helped to rebuild his shattered business. Laporterie's chain of stores, which had numbered four in 1939, was cut now to three, two in Mont-de-Marsan and one in Grenade, all struggling to break even.

"As soon as I saw that man, I knew my troubles were over," Goertz said. Willingly, he and Heyl both went to Laporterie. To this day, Goertz says, "He was my friend. He saved my life." Speaking of this, Laporterie nonchalantly told a friend, "*Comme ça on n'a pas d'ennemis.*" (That way, you have no enemies.)

This was the story throughout Landes and in many other parts of France. When the surviving prisoners were let out of Labouheyre to work on the farms, the farmers were so shocked by "the men who looked like nails" that they asked for no work at first but simply fed the men in silence.

CHAPTER 14

What Is Peace?

Enjoy the war, the peace is going to be terrible.
— graffito on a wall in Berlin, spring 1945

AFTER THE WAR, everything was worse. Most of the victors were crippled, most of the defeated devastated. For the Germans, the war continued, worse than ever, as the Allies took their revenge in the camps, confiscated food and land, drove fifteen million people, mainly women and children, from their homes in the east, and starved civilians in the remainder of Germany. The Germans were in such bad shape that the renowned British publisher Victor Gollancz cried out against it in a compassionate pamphlet entitled "Leaving Them to Their Fate: the Ethics of Starvation."[1] "The plain fact is that . . . we are starving the German people. . . . We prefer their death to our inconvenience." Gollancz was a reliable witness who not only had seen Germany in 1946 but had suffered directly from German anti-Semitism himself.

The American columnist Dorothy Thompson, widely read in the United States, condemned Allied policies in 1947 for their hypocritical brutality:

. . . Herr Sauckel was condemned and hanged [at Nuremberg] because he brought foreign workers to Germany and impressed them as slave labor . . . [France] with our consent and connivance and in defiance of the Geneva Convention, has been employing [Germans] as slave labor under the same definition as that used against Herr Sauckel in Nuremberg. . . . But do only a handful of people see that if, having defeated Germany, we accept for ourselves Hitler's standards, Hitler has conquered?[2]

The long strain of the war told on the Laporteries as it told on everyone else in Europe. What M. and Mme Laporterie were going through resulted as much from history as from character. They had seen the suffering and death of too many innocent people whom they were trying to save. To fail with one was to feel the burden of a death they might have prevented. Like Yaeche, they lost their joie de vivre, almost to the point of apathy. The young men they had known in Grenade who were now dead, or the dead families of Bordeaux, haunted them. Worse than the unanswerable question "Why?" was the recurring memory of terror: the bullets and flames hitting the houses of Grenade, the suspicious officer holding out the phone saying "Talk," the Gestapo men coming along the street toward La Petite Maison. . . . After the news of the German death camps was published, they shuddered for Sarah Yaeche's parents on the train like the boys from Grenade, standing for days in the heat and the rain with no food, while people fell dead at their feet.

Mme Laure, a small, vital woman who had always supported her beloved Raoul, with a shoulder to the back of a cart in the mud, or standing long days behind the counter, or facing her German lodger every day with sangfroid after feeding her refugees, had never lacked in energy or courage until the strain was over. Now she lost her drive. Years went by before she got back the élan she had always possessed. To her now even her once-beloved Raoul was "my executioner," as she said with a rueful smile. She shrank into herself, sadder and weaker for what she had been through.

Henri Vinet was still bubbling with good spirits despite everything. He went to Germany to buy at an auction a Mercedes that had belonged to Hitler. He drove it back triumphantly through Landes, honking Hitler's horn, laughing with delight. The car advertised his hotel for him as he sold rides to help pay for it.

Drinking with Laporterie one night, Vinet was uncharacteristically abstracted, thinking of the young men from Landes now going off to fight in Vietnam or Algeria. When Laporterie asked what he was thinking, Vinet said, "Who would have thought when we were born that we would live long enough for three big wars?"

Men in public life usually neglect their families, who resent it. So it was with the Laporteries for some years after the war, as Raoul tried to rebuild his shattered business, improve Bascons after the wartime neglect and continue his political career.

He received death threats from the communists, which were followed by scandalous stories spreading from Bascons. His enemies managed to prevent him from getting some of the honors that were due to him. His influential friend Jean Pouzelgues supported him for the Légion d'honneur, but Laporterie was mysteriously turned down, though other men who merited it less were given the prestigious award. Pouzelgues told Laporterie he could not understand it. Laporterie despised the vainglory of the latter-day Resistance heroes who were claiming honors now that the only danger they were in was the risk of being denounced as charlatans. Laporterie at first said very little about what he had done himself, but his pride demanded he receive recognition. Others were becoming well known, as writers built the myth of the Resistance on the reality of the Resistance. The famous Colonel Rémy, Resistance historian, wrote in praise of the heroic deeds of Mayor Lemée in a series of books that became famous. But when Laporterie wrote to Colonel Arnould in Paris, asking to be recognized for his work in Arnould's *réseau*, the reply was curt: be satisfied with what you have. What Laporterie had done for the refugees remained almost unknown in France.

In politics, however, his successes continued. He was elected many times as mayor of Bascons and several times as *conseiller d'arrondissement* after the war, but was twice defeated narrowly when he ran for the *préfecture*. Both times it appeared that he might have succeeded if he had had more time or money to devote to the campaign.

The friendship between Yaeche and Laporterie came to mean a great deal to both men as they tried, with each other's help, to restore the prosperous order they had both known before. Yaeche, with Elias, a friend in Bordeaux, and several others, wrote a joint letter to the biggest newspaper in Bordeaux describing what Laporterie and the Basconnais had done. Yaeche told the Grand Rabbi of Bordeaux about Laporterie's work, and his name was inscribed in a book of honor in Bordeaux memorializing the men and women who had saved refugees from Hitler.

Soon after the war, Irène Laporterie married Roger Duvignau, who had been for four years a prisoner in Germany. He had gone away a well-educated, handsome, debonair young man. He came back aged, sticklike, apathetic. As Laure had done with Raoul, Irène helped Roger back to health. Her daughter Nicole was born in 1950, one of three grandchildren for Raoul and Laure.

La Petite Maison was in poor shape financially after the war, but the morale in the main store in Mont-de-Marsan was high. For Goertz and Heyl, who had spent most of their adult lives as soldiers or prisoners, La Petite Maison was a marvelous place.

The other workers, especially Mme Hortense, soon made them feel comfortable. She was an easygoing, capable woman who doted on Raoul, keeping the shop running despite shortages of labor, cloth and electricity. She immediately liked shy young Hans Goertz, patiently teaching him what she needed. At first his wounded hand bothered him, but he had his old facility back within a few weeks because he was determined not to disappoint Laporterie. The thought of returning to Labouheyre, or Daugnague, or Buglose, anywhere on that trail of death horrified him, so there was nothing at La Petite Maison that he would not do, or try to do.

Hitler had sent Hans Goertz and Adam Heyl to rid the east of communists and other inferior types with the promise that when they returned, they would live in a Europe cleansed of Jews, Gypsies and communists. Inferior semi-Aryans, such as the French, would slave for the Reich, which would last a thousand years. Yet now, two years after the Reich had collapsed in its twelfth year, Goertz and Heyl, barely out of slavery themselves, worked for a gentlemanly Frenchman who had saved their lives, a Frenchwoman whom they adored and an elegant Jew who helped them. Friquet — Oppenheimer — who liked Mont-de-Marsan and Laporterie so much that he settled there after the war, continued as Laporterie's private secretary. He also helped to translate for the two Germans, who had suffered even more than he had. A second Jew in the store was Quilbeuf, the young assistant sent by Yaeche from Bordeaux to help Laporterie get his business going again after the war.

Mme Hortense gave Heyl and Goertz food, as well as lessons in French and English, so they were soon healthy and conversing fairly freely with their fellow workers. Laporterie and Goertz exchanged little by way of reminiscences of prison-camp life. Linked to the pain they had both suffered was shame about the cause, the cruelty of both nations. The deeper the shame, the more violent the passion needed to deny responsibility. But it was passion, as Hitler had said, that urged men to war.

Goertz didn't want to make trouble now that he and Heyl were free: Laporterie didn't want to find out any more than he had already seen in their exhausted eyes and bodies. Like all the French, he didn't want to know anything for fear of finding out everything.

So strong in France was the myth of France's civilized nature, so rigid the rejection of all guilt, that Le Monde, making a survey of the prisoners' work program as it was ending, could say only that the captivity was "a remarkable human experience in many respects,"[3] which was then ending "silently, and almost with indifference." The paper pointed with relief to the financial profit shown by France on the remarkable human experience. This profit was made through the labor of prisoners who, if they were paid at all, had to work six months for enough to buy a tube of toothpaste.[4] Most of the prisoners were paid nothing. On the subject of food and health, Le Monde said: "This was one of the most important and debatable problems. . . . At the beginning of their captivity, there was a great food shortage in France. [The Germans] could not be granted higher rations than the Frenchmen received." This article appeared more than a year after the issuance of a report[5] by Mr. Meyer, the chief delegate of the International Red Cross, who had succeeded Pradervand. Having inspected all the prison camps and prisons for German prisoners of war in France in 1947, he reported that "the conditions were of the worst sort. There was little or no medical care; the diet averaged below 1000 calories per day and the sanitary conditions were definitely of the poorest sort."

The reference to the food shortage reveals an interesting flaw in the myth. Enough French people suspected what was happening in the camps that a second myth was invented to deny what was not covered by the first. The second myth was the world food shortage. In fact, there was no lethal food shortage in the Allied nations after the war. More wheat and more maize (corn) were produced in 1945 than had been produced in 1939 in West Germany, France, England, Canada and the United States combined. There was a slight drop in potato production. The starvation of Goertz and the other Germans was a policy, not a shortage.[6]

Goertz's experience on emerging from the French army camps into French civilian life was repeated all over the country. From hatred, neglect and death, the prisoners were transported in a few minutes, in a few meters, to forgiveness and life. When the gates of the camp opened for these men, they entered the world of families, of women, of children, on farms, in small towns, villages, in small enterprises, where they encountered kindnesses they had almost forgotten, which they never forgot again. For one of Goertz's fellow prisoners, Werner Steckelings, the experience was so passionate that for the rest of his life he refused to discuss the atrocities committed against the prisoners without first impressing on his audience the wonderful kindness of the French civilians. For more than forty years he has gone on visiting and writing to the family near Lyon who took him in and brought him back to life after he had almost died in the camps.

The prisoners did not speak out sooner because there was obviously no point. Besides, the horror of what they had been through left them speechless. Neither Goertz nor Heyl said anything of the French camps to Laporterie. It was not until forty years had passed that Goertz said anything to a writer, and then only to set the kindness of Laporterie into perspective. Heyl refused to talk to anyone ever again about the camps.

To many of the French, success is not worth a short life. But Laporterie forgot this rule in his haste to restore his business to what it had been before. He was soon struggling in a confusion of clothing styles that had never existed before.

Once Christian Dior had brought out the New Look in Paris in the late forties, women all over the world accepted him as dictator of fashion, setting styles, especially skirt lengths. Then Yves Saint-Laurent, Dior's protégé, eliminated the affair between the individual and the tailor, which had always been the source of fashion. Now suddenly design became mass, and tailoring, except for the rich, was unnecessary, even for men. Theodor Zeldin, a sympathetic, accurate observer of France, wrote: "The socialist President of the Republic dresses exactly like his aristocratic predecessor. . . . All the members of his cabinet parade in dark suits; even the communists are indistinguishable."[7]

What this meant to La Petite Maison was that the foundation of the business was threatened. Excellent and expensive tailoring for individuals was on the way out; ready-to-wear was on the way in. The French, contrary to the general impression, have never paid much attention to fashion. They spend less of their income on clothing than any other European nation. They are conservative in style and modest in outlay.[8]

Like all successful men facing unexpected trouble, Laporterie thought there was something wrong with the way he was doing things, not with the things he set out to do. So he responded too slowly to the permanent change in taste. The business faltered. He had to close all but two stores eventually, leaving only one in Mont-de-Marsan and the one in Grenade, where he lived. Frustrated and bewildered, he was short-tempered with his family. He quarreled so violently with Laure that Irène and her daughter Nicole were afraid. He was often away.

Just before an election campaign in Bascons, enemies there suddenly accused him of using public funds to his own advantage. Among the accusers were several old friends or allies well known in the village. Trial after expensive trial ensued. Laporterie lost at Pau, but won in the final judgment, in the Cour de Cassation at Paris. Poorer and sadder but never bitter, Laporterie went on campaigning for office. He was vindicated a second time when he was reelected mayor, and he went on with his many interests — in the bull-dancing and bullfighting of Landes, and in campaigns against tuberculosis, cancer and other diseases. He also ran a fund to refurbish the village church and to help restore Bascons, which won a national prize as the most beautiful village in France. With the help of his devoted Irène and son-in-law, Roger, he gradually rebuilt his clothing business until it began to provide a comfortable livelihood once more for the family.

The days of his neglect were now ending, as well. After he ceased to stand for election in Bascons, he was elected honorary mayor. Writers were at last beginning to take an interest in the unknown honorable France that he represented, along with the modest heroes of Le Chambon and many other places. Laure had completely recovered her energy along with her joie de vivre, and her indulgent love for "mon bourreau" (my burden). They were comfortable with each other and with their grandchildren and great grandchildren, who all lived nearby and frequently visited.

The famous Resistance historian Henri Amouroux discovered Laporterie through the journalist Georges Dubos of Mont-de-Marsan. Dubos had long stood in awe of Laporterie's high-spirited defiance, so he introduced the historian to the man who had made history. Amouroux wrote a brief account of Laporterie's work as a passeur for his book La vie des Français sous l'Occupation. In 1976, the director of the memorial institute called Yad Vashem in Israel asked Laporterie to accept the Medal of the Just, struck by the institute to honor all those who had helped Jews to escape the Holocaust of the Second World War. In his acceptance speech at the Israeli embassy in Paris, Laporterie explained in public for the first time the most important thing he had ever done. Behind locked steel doors in the heavily guarded embassy, he said, "If I was able to help numerous Jews to pass through the holes of the net that was set for them and to find them refuges which put them out of the reach of the Germans, my action was dictated above all by humane sentiments for beings worse off than I — followed, as they were, by the implacable and monstrous hate of the occupying force — but also by my absolute refusal to submit to and accept the conditions of life which were imposed on us, and by a desire, a violent need, for revenge and struggle against despotism and tyranny."

Laporterie combined compassion with passion. The beauty he sees in others is the beauty that shines from his own face. So he is intense without moralizing. Hans Deichmann, a German who saved people in defiance of the Nazis, has said of this kind of behavior:

> I wasn't a moralist. I fully enjoyed everything beautiful that came within my grasp and I felt no remorse. Yet I also had a constant perception of the horror all around. I once returned to Rome from Auschwitz, full of indescribable terror, only to fall in love with a young Roman woman a few days later. While I was embracing her, I continued to think of Auschwitz and of what I could do to help stop the evil. I was 'playing' simultaneously with terribly serious things and with light-hearted, amusing ones, and only by approaching the serious things, too, as a game, with a sort of lucid nonchalance, day by day, did I manage to accomplish anything at all.[9]

Such people did not enter evil, by not allowing evil to enter them.

In the audience at the embassy was American writer Peter Hellman, who had come upon Laporterie while researching a book on the subject of the people honored at Yad Vashem. Hellman was charmed by this forceful, humorous man. Laporterie agreed to let Hellman use his archives at Grenade to prepare a short chapter in his book, *Avenue of the Righteous*. In it Hellman says Raoul Laporterie is "a man who steers away from philosophy . . . but beneath the breezy charm in which he likes to bathe his exploits runs a subcurrent of pure, fierce and highly focused feeling for his obligations to others and to himself."

The Yad Vashem Institute, in offering the medal, had told Laporterie that it was customary for recipients to plant a carob tree beside the Avenue of the Just at the institute on a hillside near Jerusalem. Unfortunately the institute could not offer the fare for the voyage. So Hellman, without telling Laporterie, called some friends in New York. Would they chip in to buy an airline ticket for this man who had saved so many people? The money was offered through the Israeli embassy in Paris to Laporterie, who accepted.

So one day in 1980, Raoul Laporterie stood in a pearl-gray suit from the Castel family on a hot stony hillside in a land he had often dreamed of, as had the people he had saved. There, with a man from the New World who was writing his story, accompanied by Esther Levy and Rivka Cassutto, two sisters he had saved from the death camps, he turned the soil of the Promised Land to plant a tree in honor of the righteous life he had lived.

Nine years later, the French government at last awarded him the honor he prized above all others — the Légion d'honneur as a soldier of France.

Epilogue
The Modest Millions

HUNDREDS OF thousands of people like Laporterie did not abandon the ideals of France when the government of France abandoned them. In this last half of the twentieth century, when war no longer works, when autocracies fall by the decay of faith, when power shrinks from purpose so that everyone wonders about the worth of government, it is marvelously refreshing to see flourishing in the ruins of France ordinary goodness in a man, a town, that outlasted the tyrant and his empire.

Many were the French people who in June of 1940 felt the shame of defeat personally, because they knew they had contributed to it. Philippe Pétain, in June 1940 offering his person like a savior to France, foreshadowed the de Gaulle who paraded himself without any foreign allies through Paris in 1944, trying to create the illusion that France had liberated herself under his leadership. In those ecstatic days, because victory meant liberation, liberation came to mean victory. Whoever was credited for liberation was awarded the palm of victory and the right to govern. France having lost the war, de Gaulle found it necessary to proclaim that France had won the war. Under de Gaulle. As he walked into Notre-Dame, he might as well have spread his arms and said, *Après le deluge, moi.*

To prove that the glory of France continued under de Gaulle, myths were created, books written, truth suppressed, documents destroyed and new wars begun. In 1945, de Gaulle begged money and arms from the Americans for an expeditionary force to Indochina to drive out Ho Chi Minh's communists. So at the end of one catastrophe, de Gaulle prepared another for his country.

"That was the policy of de Gaulle," the Quaker Gilbert Lesage said in Paris in 1989. "There's a psychological warp in it that contradicts truth, but public opinion has no sense of truth." Recently an educated middle-class Frenchman assured me that France had won the Second World War. Astounded, I pointed out that France asked for an armistice in 1940, that she was occupied for four and a half years. No matter, the Resistance, with the help of the Allies, had liberated his country. He had memorized statistics of the numbers of bridges blown, trains destroyed. This to him was a complete story, because it included difficult truth while annulling it. The historians to this day continue the game. Jean-Pierre Rioux wrote recently of *"La France victorieuse"* in 1945.[1] Probably very few people wholeheartedly believe this, but very few people are willing either to challenge the notion, or to show any interest in whatever it is that this myth has been set up to hide. Thus they hang between the lie and the void.

To this day in France, most students are taught nothing about the French people who risked death to save hundreds of thousands of men, women and children from Nazi terror during the Second World War. Nevertheless the ideals live on, like fire in the roots of the forest. They burn among the *Français moyens,* the ordinary people of France, especially in the villages, farms and small towns of the country, among those not rich or glamorous, the modest millions who make up the largest part of the citizenry of most Western countries. The many among the modest millions who saved others during the war said little or nothing afterward because they did not want to vaunt themselves. Not only was self-promotion immodest, but it contradicted to some degree the self-abnegation inherent in what they had done. For many of the saviors it was normal, not heroic, to help others. The true heroes were the grotesque Nazis, heroes of evil. Praise was therefore out of place for modest people who thought they had acted naturally and normally. This is the banality of good. Anyone who adores it cannot understand it. In forty-five years, Gilbert Lesage never spoke or wrote of what he did on behalf of Jews during the war; others have described his work in books and at Yad Vashem, the museum at Jerusalem, which honors the just.

How many French Jews, and how many Jewish refugees in France did the people of France save from murder during the war? Of approximately 330,000 who had been in France in 1940, about 250,000 were saved. Probably all of them were helped at some point by French Christians, atheists and agnostics who risked the death camps themselves in order to help their fellow citizens. Because each Jewish family was usually lodged or fed by several French families at some point, and received illegal papers from officials, it is quite possible that for every Jew saved, one to four French people risked deportation or death. Thus, possibly 250,000 to 1,000,000 French people risked their lives to help the strangers at the gate. In no other country of Europe did so many risk so much for their neighbors. In no other country was there such blind forgetting of the good things people do.

Of the approximately 330,000 Jews in France in 1940,[2] about 130,000 to 140,000 were not French but refugees.[3] A total of about 80,000 people died, mainly in deportation to the east, a few in French camps. Of these 80,000, about 24,000 were French citizens, the remainder refugees. Thus the Nazis managed to kill from thirty-nine to forty-two percent of the refugees then in France. The difference between the two rates of saving is extraordinary, for only about thirteen percent of the French Jews died. Of the "French" Jews, approximately 7000 were young children of refugee Jews, who were extremely difficult to save because they were automatically swept up along with their parents. Some of the most poignant stories of the war in France involved the deportation of children. If they are subtracted from the 24,000 French deported, that number shrinks to about 17,000, meaning that the Jews' fellow citizens had been able to help protect more than 93 percent. The explanation is complex. The French were able to protect such a large number of their Jewish fellow citizens because these citizens were at first not hunted or imprisoned like the others. They were far less noticeable than the refugees, and they had friends and relatives who could help them. The refugees, mostly held in camps, treated like friends of fascism although they had fled it, lacking relatives and friends, speaking accented French, outside not only the French community but even for a while outside the Jewish community, were much more exposed than the French citizens. For many of the long-established Jews of Bordeaux, thoroughly integrated with their Christian neighbors, these foreigners speaking their peculiar French were a severe embarrassment, who would soon endanger them. Integration with them was out of the question: "They are far-distant cousins," said the integrated Jews, forgetting that their own ancestors had been chased out of Spain to haven in France during the Spanish pogroms of the fifteenth and sixteenth centuries. They did not think these strangers from the east had any special right to the privileges that they themselves enjoyed. They looked down on their far-distant cousins because they were in minor trades, practicing a strange liturgy in a weird accent. To most of the Bordelais Sephardim, with a few exceptions, they were not welcome.[4]

Many of these refugees were put straight into camps by the government in 1939 or 1940, because there might have been spies among them, or perhaps simply because, like the Spanish refugees before them, they were a nuisance and no one knew what else to do with them. In camps such as Gurs near Pau in the south, there were over 16,000 internees in the summer of

1940, all subjected to humiliating discomforts and deprivation of food and medicine soon leading to an obscenely high death rate.

One of the most active of all the saviors, Madeleine Barot, arrived there in September 1940 on a mission to help the Protestant inmates. Barot had a simple way of dealing with the suspicious bureaucrats staring over their paper blockade at the entrance to misery. She made no application. She asked for no official permission. Her calm voice rattled no Evian bottles on the desks of the mighty. In Protestant tweeds, she marched sturdily to the gate at Gurs beside the Protestant minister. At her suggestion, the minister asked the guard for permission to bring his assistant in to do some social work while he went about his regular pastoral round. The guard hesitated, for he was well aware of the huge cement tanks of feces onto which the prisoners had to climb on slippery ladders to evacuate themselves. Sometimes, perched on the edge, they lost their seating and took an unplanned bath. Barot, serenely determined, mounted on her sensible shoes, gave promise of being able to countenance this without giving trouble, and perhaps even of calming some of the inmates, understandably restless under this treatment. She was permitted to enter that day, and the day after, until she was walking in and out with a cheery *bonjour* to the guards whose work she was doing her best to undo. She gained access for other groups, too, such as the Quakers, to do relief work, and organized still other groups to make the relief more effective. She attended not just to the Protestant rite, but also the Catholics, Jews and those who professed belief in no god in this apparently godforsaken place. All together, these were "the scum of the earth," as the inmate Arthur Koestler said after he left Gurs.

There were in Gurs approximately 800 Protestants, about 800 to 1000 Catholics, about 2000 communists and other political internees; the remainder were Jewish refugees from Germany, Austria, Czechoslovakia, Poland. Besides Gurs, there was a total of thirteen camps in the south — Rivesaltes, Le Vernet, Milles, Agde, Argèles, Noë, St-Cyprien and five others — and five temporary holding camps.[5] Raoul Laporterie, Madeleine Barot and others managed to secure the release of some prisoners from these camps, but the great majority were still there at the time of the Wannsee conference in January 1942, when the Final Solution was toasted by Nazi officers in front of a fireplace in a Berlin suburb. Vichy, under the thumb of the Nazis, feebly cooperated when the orders came to ship these people out.

With the help of French friends, many of the refugees managed to avoid both the Nazis and the Vichy police in the summer of 1942. When the Nazis decided on the roundup known as the *Vel d'hiver* in July in Paris, there were approximately 28,000 refugees shown by name on police lists as living in the region, but when the roundup was over, about 15,000 of these people, warned by sympathizers, some of whom apparently must have been within the Paris police, had escaped.[6] Most of these went south; virtually all of them went into hiding in the countryside, helped by organizations headed by such people as Madeleine Barot and Gilbert Lesage. A few managed to live out the war in hiding in Paris.[7]

"There were enormous numbers of people helping the Jews," said Lesage, who knew many of them.[8] On the other hand, as Serge Klarsfeld has written " . . . the Nazis [had] the active complicity of Vichy to apply the Final Solution of the Jewish problem."[9]

These statements, apparently in conflict, are both true. Inside the government of Vichy, an important number of officials complied with orders originating in Berlin to round up foreign Jews residing in France for deportation to the east. The probable range of motives was political conviction, blind obedience, anti-Semitism or fear of losing a job. Outside the city of Vichy itself, at lower levels of the hierarchy of the Vichy government, many officials secretly resisted while pretending to comply; it seems likely that the farther away the officials were from the city, the more they resisted the racist orders. Those who saved refugees had to have tremendously strong motivation because they were risking their lives; those who complied with the Nazis needed only inertia mixed with a little self-interest. For most, there may have been no race hatred at all, just moral apathy. But generally the French had sympathy for all those who were persecuted by the Nazis. "More than ever, the Jewish masses of France are loyal to the people of France. They know that all are the victims of the same oppressor," said one Jewish clandestine organization called Solidarité.[10] "No French person I asked ever refused to help a Jew," said Madeleine Barot.[11]

British intelligence experts, informed by a network of spies in France, reported a "considerable number"[12] of French "military and police officers in southern France who had refused to carry out orders for the arrest of Jews."[13] The British concluded: "It seems beyond doubt that the French population in general strongly disapproves of the campaign. . . ."[14] "The majority of the Aryan population continued to show anti-German, and even Gaullist sentiment, for many. . . ."[15] All this disapproval worried the Germans and the officials at Vichy so much that they began to hold their roundups at night "like bandits so as not to enrage the general population."[16]

One of the men placed between the mighty of Vichy and the mayors and prefects was the regional chief of police of Toulouse, Charles M. Heyl, who repeatedly warned local Jews of projected roundups, thus saving many lives at the risk of his own.[17] Others quietly shifted categories and documents so as to let more refugees escape from France. Some deportation orders of 1941 emanating from Berlin, going via Paris to Vichy, first met opposition from a strange source — Germans in the occupation forces in France. Kreiskommandant Major Henkel recommended in the summer of 1941 that 150 Jews recently evacuated from the sensitive coastal region not be retransferred to other *départements* of France, but be allowed to emigrate. Berlin refused, apparently deciding their fate — internment, to be followed by the train to Auschwitz. But some of the Jewish refugees escaped anyway, even long after the Wannsee conference, which had condemned them all. The German consul in Casablanca wrote a letter to Berlin in March 1942, reporting that over 1600 Jewish émigrés had recently passed through on several ships going from Spain, Portugal and Vichy France to North America, having been helped by the Jewish aid agency in Paris.[18] The consul was exercised partly because some hundreds of these were young men en route to Canada to join the Royal Canadian Air Force. The German complaints about these émigrés, who were leaving with the help of Vichy and the Spanish governments, and the cooperation of the Dutch and Polish governments-in-exile and the Canadian government, carried on at least until July, when another 500 émigrés traveled via Casablanca en route to Canada and the U.S. The German consul actually visited one of the ships, the *St. Thomas*, then commented, "The emigrants . . . seemed to be well cared for and healthy. The percentage of German Jews was relatively small." He was well aware of the details of the operation, which he described to Berlin: "The Poles were headed to Canada, where they will join the air force. The passage of these Poles was arranged by a Jewish aid organization and the "Polish Office," under an arrangement between the Sikorski government and the Vichy government. The Spanish government, at the request of the Vichy government, made no difficulties about issuing visas permitting these Poles of military age to [go to Canada to] fight for the enemy." Most of the émigrés, he added, were from Central Europe, Germany and France. These letters, describing the frequent departures that he was helpless to prevent, ended with the plaintive note, "Please advise the military authorities," which contrasts very oddly with the picture we have of Vichy helping the Germans in their relentless pursuit of the refugees.

In Le Chambon-sur-Lignon, a village high in the mountains west of the Rhône south of Lyon, strange events were occurring in the middle of the war. The Germans were hunting down children while their armies were being destroyed in Russia; Frenchmen and women in this tiny village were saving those same children. Among the saviors of the children was a man charged with their destruction.

His name was Julius Schmahling, a German army major who was stationed at Le Puy, about forty kilometers from Le Chambon. As the *Kommandant* of the Wehrmacht for the whole large Haute-Loire region, he knew when the roundups of Jews were planned; in fact, he must have helped to plan them himself. This region, stuffed with tough Maquisards, was difficult and dangerous for Schmahling, which made it even harder for him to do what he now did — warn the Chambonnais when one of his own raids was about to happen.[19]

The Protestant pastor of Le Chambon, André Trocmé, was working beside his parishioners, coordinating their efforts to save thousands of Jews. The refugees were fed, sheltered and protected throughout the war in the homes of the villagers and nearby farmers. From time to time, the phone would ring in Trocmé's study. Trocmé heard a voice with a German accent say, "You will have visitors today." Then the line would go dead. The first time this happened, the alert Trocmé figured out the meaning right away. He warned his villagers, who put their guests into hiding. When the police arrived the next day, not one Jew was found. After every call from Schmahling, it was the same. Only one refugee was ever caught, a schoolboy who was taken alone in a bus intended for dozens of children. Many thousands, probably more than 5000 people all told, were taken in, fed, sheltered and saved by the Chambonnais during four years. All this they did openly, never denying their actions in the face of Nazi or Vichy terror. Faced with prison himself, Pastor Trocmé one day said to the visiting police, "Yes, it's true that we have Jews here, but we will not give them up to you, because we know what will happen to them."[20] Trocmé was arrested, imprisoned for several months, but survived.

The camp commanders had a macabre dependency on the refugees, for it was on the refugees that their jobs depended. Without prisoners, there would be no warm and tidy office for the camp commander. Thus the "scum of the earth" had for the commanders at least the cold value of the miser's hoard. The Grand Rabbi of Strasbourg, the warmhearted René Hirschler, a smiling man with an unconvincing beard fringing his slightly pudgy chin, was alert to this symbiosis in misery, which he exploited masterfully in the summer of 1942. The Nazis informed Vichy that they wanted to deport 20,000 people to help "build the new Jewish state in the east," as the euphemism of the day had it. Sympathizers within the Vichy government warned Hirschler, providing him with copies of the orders, which contained six interesting categories of people who could be exempted. Hirschler, impressively French with his air of good living, his beret raked down over his left ear, in French army uniform with religious insignia peeping out between two buttons, conferred immediately with the officials. It was obvious that newborn babies would not be much use in heaving up the girders of the new state in the east. Nor could much mixing of cement be counted on among the pregnant women or blinded one-armed war veterans. All these people would take up valuable space in the trains, detracting from the war effort of the Fatherland, while at the same time consuming scarce food. Vichy, stuck with the notion of the Jewish state, yielded, allowing Hirschler to double the number of categories, until they provided escape hatches for nearly everyone in the camps. Hirschler now had to get the word quickly from the city of Vichy to the people in the camps chiefly in the south, but he could not risk frightening the government into a change of heart by sending the news openly in telegrams, letters or even by phone to his helpers. So he had to send runners to the south, by train, individually to each camp, to deliver the news clandestinely through sympathizers, such as Barot. All this had to be organized in three days, and it was. When the deportation orders from Vichy began arriving in places such as Gurs, the applications for regularization or change of status were already piled high, many even approved already. "The chaplains [including many rabbis] were watchful: they delayed the departure of infants, of the pregnant, the old, the war veterans; they demanded that the camp commanders read their directives carefully; they fought toe to toe with the surlier commanders. They thus stopped the deportation of hundreds and probably thousands of Jews, for when the sad accounting was done, instead of 20,000 gone as originally envisaged by Vichy, only around 13,000 were gone."[21]

There is a farm in the south of France among low hills that swell up to the Pyrénées. Here in red brick buildings set around a central courtyard, sunny on the day we visited, live the Daubas family, father Valentin Jean Louis, his wife, the children and grandchildren, growing vines, grain, vegetables, kiwi fruit. They are at peace now as they were in 1942, when the Germans suddenly invaded the region, driving Jews ahead of them like sheep before wolves. The Jewish Dessauer family sought refuge in the village of Casterat nearby. In the village, they were too exposed to stay more than a short time, so Valentin Daubas invited them to stay with him and his family on their farm. Daubas, in 1989 still a tough man with no nonsense about him, blue-eyed and horny-handed, said, "I was sad at their fate." He fed and sheltered them for many months, risking himself and his whole family. In the end, the Dessauers were saved. At peace then, at peace now, Daubas said in 1989, "If I had it to do over, I'd do it again."

Notes

Chapter 1 / **Gallia Est Omnis Divisa in Partes Tres**

1. "All Gaul (France) is divided into three parts" — Julius Caesar
2. Charles de Gaulle, *The Complete War Memoirs*. New York: Da Capo Press, undated, p. 55.

Chapter 2 / **Saving the People**

1. Josef Hell, *Aufzeichnung*, ZS 640. München: Institut fur Zeitgeschichte, 1922, p. 6. Quoted in Gerald Fleming, *Hitler and the Final Solution*. Berkeley: University of California Press, 1984, p. 29.
2. Pétain's government at Vichy remained nominally responsible for certain civil affairs through all of France, including the German-Occupied zone.
3. Michel Slitinsky, *L'Affaire Papon*. Paris: Editions Alain Moreau, 1983, p. 43.
4. Ibid., pp. 43-4.
5. Ibid., p. 55.

Chapter 3 / **Growing Up Landais**

1. D. J. Goodspeed, *Ludendorff, Genius of World War I*. Toronto: Macmillan of Canada, 1966, p. 211.
2. Jean-Paul Sartre, *The War Diaries*. New York: Pantheon Books, 1984, p. 64.
3. De Gaulle, op. cit., pp. 6-7.
4. Speech by Curé Luttenbacher: notes in the archives of Raoul Laporterie, Grenade.
5. Sartre, op. cit., p. 32.
6. Archives of Raoul Laporterie, Grenade.

Chapter 5 / **Spreading the Net**

1. Henri Amouroux, *Quatre ans d'histoire de France.* Paris: Hachette, 1966, p. 91. Passage translated by James Bacque.
2. Richard Cobb, *French and Germans, Germans and French.* Hanover: University Press of New England, 1983, p. 103.
3. Henri Amouroux, *La vie des Français sous l'Occupation.* Paris: Fayard, 1961. Passage translated by James Bacque.
4. A. Hitler, *Mein Kampf.* Boston: Houghton Mifflin, 1943, p. 140.

Chapter 6 / **The Worst Winter of the War**

1. Slitinsky, op. cit., p. 72.
2. The Germans had about 10,000 agents in France, and La Milice (the Vichy police) at least 100,000 members. Cobb, op. cit., p. 103.

Chapter 7 / **A Dangerous Comedy**

1. M. Laporterie was unable to complete this story with the name of the *passeur* and details about the settlement because to reveal these would cause embarrassment to people still alive in the region.
2. Nuremberg trial information paraphrased and quoted from *Justice at Nuremberg*, by Robert E. Conot. New York: Harper and Row, 1983, p. 258.
3. *Colonel* in many cases at the time did not denote a rank but was a term of affectionate respect.

Chapter 8 / **Vive de Gaulle**

1. Henri Amouroux, *La vie des Français sous l'Occupation*, p. 170.
2. Colonel Rémy, *La Résistance en Aquitaine.* Genève: Editions Famot, 1974, p. 110. Passage translated by James Bacque.
3. The editors were not part of the Mouvement Franc Tireur, which was not communist. Footnote thanks to Odette Guitard, former professor of history at the Université d'Aix-en-Provence.
4. Geneva correspondent of the *National Zeitung*, November 30, 1942, quoted in Amouroux, *La vie des Français sons l'occupation, p.* 548.
5. Gerald Fleming, *Hitler and the Final Solution.* Berkeley: University of California Press, 1984, pp. 53-4.

6. For the full story, see the Epilogue.
7. Quoted and paraphrased from *Choices in Vichy France* by John F. Sweets. Oxford: Oxford University Press, 1986.

Chapter 9 / The Joy of Goodness

1. Amouroux, *La vie des Francais sous l'Occupation*, p. 157.
2. Author's interview with Charles Read, Head of Mission for American Friends Service Committee in France, General Oversight, 1946.
3. Slitinsky, op. cit., pp. 87-90.
4. Ibid., p. 88.
5. M. Goubelle, *La Résistance dans les Landes*. La Préfecture des Landes, Mont-de-Marsan, undated.

Chapter 10 / Bauführer Laporterie

1. Jean-Pierre Azéma, *De Munich à la liberation*. Paris: Editions du Seuil, 1979, p. 214.
2. Amouroux, *Quatre ans d'histoire de France*, p. 138.
3. Staff Conference, Chiefs of Staff Committee No. 39 (Operations) of 1944. Churchill, Brooke, Portal and Andrew Cunningham. Quoted in Martin Gilbert, *Road to Victory*. Toronto: Stoddart Publishing Co. Limited, 1986, p. 677.
4. Slitinsky, op. cit., p. 137.

Chapter 12 / A Night of Liberty, a Dawn of Sorrow

1. H. R. Kedward, Basil Blackwell, *Occupied France: Collaboration and Resistance, 1940-44*. Oxford: Oxford University Press, 1985, p. 73.
2. De Gaulle, op. cit., p. 682.
3. Ibid., p. 937.

Chapter 13 / The French and American Death Camps

1. Interview with Hans Goertz in Bonn, April 1986. Also interview with Le Chanoine Jean-Baptiste St-Germain, Dax, April 1986.
2. Report of a visit to a U.S. Army prison camp for German prisoners

of war, by Col. James B. Mason, MC-USA (Ret.) and Col. Charles A. Beasley, MC-USA (Ret.) in "Medical Arrangements for Prisoners of War en Masse," originally published in *The Medical Surgeon*, Vol. 107, No. 6, December 1950, p. 437.

3. Interview with A. Berger, Mulheim, West Germany, May 1986.

4. Interview with Heinz T., Paris, June 1986.

5. Heinz T. has asked to remain anonymous.

6. Interview with Heinz T., Paris, June 1986.

7. Pradervand to de Gaulle, September 1945. Box 7 P40, Vincennes.

8. Lieutenant Soubeiray, Third Algerians, to his commanding officer, September 3, 1945. Box 11P60, Vincennes.

9. Henry W. Dunning, American Red Cross, to State Department, September 25, 1945. In 740.62114/ 9-2545 CS/LE, State Department Archives, Washington.

10. Lt. Col de Champvallier to General Billotte, August 30, 1945. Various complaints and reports by French officers such as Captain Julien, Lieutenants Himmeur and Soubeiray are contained in Boxes 11P60, 11P165 and 7P40; also in the French Military Archives at Vincennes, Paris.

11. *Le Figaro*, Paris, September 22 and 29, 1945.

12. Memo of Eisenhower to AGWAR October 1945. Photocopy in Bundesarchiv, Koblenz.

13. Jefferson Caffery to State, Paris, October 13, 1945. In State Department records, U.S. National Archives. 740.62114/10-1345.

14. Interview with Francis Vaudelon et al. in Thorée-les-Pins, May 1986.

15. Interview with M. Cazaux of Buglose, April 1986.

16. Notes of meeting held under M. Jacquinot, December 1945. Box 7P40, Vincennes.

17. A list of some of the dead at Buglose with birth and death dates was compiled in the 1950s by the secretary of the *mairie*. She got the information from the painted wooden crosses in the cemetery.

18. Interview with Le Chanoine St-Germain in Dax, April 1986.

19. Archives of Raoul Laporterie, Grenade-sur-l'Adour.

20. Weekly reports of prisoners of war and DEF, TSFET to USFET signed

Larkin, in SHAEF papers, p 15 1191, U.S. National Archives. Report says 21 Army Group (British and Canadians) had 1,739,955 in hand in Germany. Author has allowed 160,045 for prisoners held in Belgium, France, Holland, Britain and Canada, plus 1,000,000 in Italy. This is a very conservative estimate.

21. The Red Cross reports are distributed through numerous boxes in the records of the foreign office in the PRO, London. The British public opinion was expressed through many people, including notably Victor Gollancz, the Lord Bishop of Chichester and *The Times*. In Canada, public opinion was expressed by Prime Minister Mackenzie King in a letter about prisoner-of-war conditions to the Foreign Office in June 1945. See James Bacque, *Other Losses*. Toronto: Stoddart Publishing Co. Limited, 1989, Chapter Ten.

22. Weekly PW and DEF reports from TSFET signed Larkin, to USFET Main, June-September 1945. In SHAEF papers, pages 15 1106 through 15 1191. Military Reference Branch, U.S. National Archives, Washington. See also Bacque, *Other Losses*.

23. See *Other Losses*, Chapter Nine, for details of how this figure was arrived at.

24. Jean-Pierre Pradervand, former International Red Cross chief delegate in France, 1945, in conversation with the author, Switzerland, October 1989.

25. Interview, J. M. Bernadet, Dax, April 1986.

26. Interview, Buglose, April 1986.

27. Reports of the local guards and prisoners indicate that the original prisoner population of Labouheyre was about 1000 maximum. One International Red Cross report (Addendum to HQ USFET Memorandum to Chief of Staff, October 9, 1945, in RG 383.6/11, NARS, Washington) says that the population of Labouheyre was 3600, but this is probably the total for several depot camps including Daugnague, Pissos and others, as well as the main camp at Labouheyre. For the purposes of this book, the population has been taken to be about 1000.

28. Archives of the town of Labouheyre, Landes, France.

Chapter 14 / **What Is Peace?**
1. Victor Gollancz, London, undated but probably 1946.
2. United States Congressional Record – Senate (1947), p. 1675.
3. *Le Monde,* January 1949, quoted in Laenderrat, Section VII, German Agency for Prisoner of War Problems, Stuttgart I. In: US section 765041, Bundesarchiv, Koblenz.
4. Interview with Heinz T., Paris, June 1986.
5. Quoted in Laenderrat, meeting of November 28, 1947, as reported by Colonel Whitted, USA. Bundesarchiv, Koblenz.
6. Bacque, op. cit.
7. Theodor Zeldin, *The French.* London: Fontana Paperbacks, 1984, pp. 313-4. Much of the preceding paragraph is paraphrased from Zeldin.
8. Ibid.
9. Hans Deichmann, quoted in *The New Yorker,* June 4, 1990.

Epilogue / **The Modest Millions**
1. Jean-Pierre Rioux, *La France de la IVeme République.* Paris: Editions du Seuil, 1980, p. 121.
2. Serge Klarsfeld, *Vichy Auschwitz.* Paris: Fayard, 1985, p 179. For the deportation figures, Klarsfeld worked from German records listing deportees train by train. No death figures kept by the Germans have survived for these deportees, so the deaths have (apparently) been estimated by subtracting the number of those who returned to France, approximately 2500, from those who departed. The returned are those who identified themselves to the French government after the war. The accuracy of this method is reduced by the fact that about two-thirds of the deportees were originally non-French refugees who had been betrayed or rounded up by the French. The surviving refugees had little or no reason to return to the country that had failed to shelter them. Any refugees not identified by the French government, including those who went to Israel or North America by routes other than France, are thus counted as dead.

3. Ibid., p. 179.
4. Slitinsky, op. cit. Slitinsky points to the exceptional work of Alexandre Felsenhardt and others to inform the Bordelais of the truth of the situation, which was that the anti-Semitism of the Nazis, if unopposed, would soon sweep away the Sephardim, too.
5. L'activité des organizations juives en France sous l'Occupation. Paris: CDJC,1983, p. 128.
6. Adam Rutkowski, La lutte des Juifs en France à l'epoque de l'Occupation. Paris: CDJC, 1975, p. 21.
7. One was Susan A., now of Toronto.
8. Interview with James Bacque, Paris, September 1989.
9. Sarraute, Tager, Schneerson and Klarsfeld. Les Juifs sous l'Occupation 1940-44. Paris: CDJC, 1982.
10. Rutkowski, op. cit. p. 60.
11. Interview with James Bacque, Paris, November 1989.
12. FO 892/115 Summary of Events, etc., 1942, PRO, London. Quoted in Sweets, op. cit.
13. Sweets, op. cit., p. 134.
14. FO 892 115 Summary of Events, etc., 1942, PRO, London. Quoted in Sweets.
15. Rutkowski, op. cit. p. 215.
16. Ibid., p. 122.
17. Erika Dessauer-Nieder, "Jewish Fates in France 1939-45." Unpublished manuscript with the author (and with the Centre de Documentation Juive Contemporaine). Dessauer-Nieder, now of Seattle, was a refugee helped by Heyl, among others.
18. Monneray, Cassin, Faure, La persecution des Juifs en France et dans les autres pays de l'ouest. Paris: Editions du Centre, 1947.
19. Philip Hallie, Griffin professor of philosophy and humanities at Wesleyan University, who wrote Lest Innocent Blood Be Shed about Le Chambon, heard a rumor in Le Chambon long after the war that a certain German named Schmahling had been the voice on the phone to Trocmé. Hallie pursued his investigations into Germany, where Schmahling had died a few years before. He found evidence enough to convince him that Schmahling was the mysterious voice

on the phone, but this version is disputed in Le Chambon itself, where some people believe that a Frenchman was behind the phone calls.

20. Hallie, *Lest Innocent Blood Be Shed*. New York: Harper and Row, 1979. The whole story of Le Chambon is told in this book.

21. *L'activité des organisations juives en France sous l'Occupation*, p. 37. The book is a compilation of the work of several authors, not named. The translation is by James Bacque.

Index

Abbeville 24
Aboressy
family 26
Adour
river 42, 111
Agde 175
Aire-sur-l'Adour 37, 83, 102,
106, 127, 129, 130, 135
Aisne 15
Aix-la-Chapelle 38
Algeria 53
Alsace 5, 15, 19, 39, 48
taken over by Germany 73
Amouroux
Henri 104, 167
Angel
family 26, 78, 143
Anglet 125
Arcachon 53, 54, 79, 123, 125
Arendt
Hannah 98, 105
Argèles 175
Arnould
Claude 51, 52, 60, 113, 162
Auschwitz 177
Austria 27, 174
Azur 125
Bad Kreuznach
U.S. camp at 148
Barcelonne 135
Barot
Madeleine 174-176, 180
Bartenheim 48, 49
Bascons 5, 19, 21, 23, 30-33,
35-37, 40, 44, 45, 48, 59, 65,
70, 72-76, 78, 79, 81, 86, 91,
109, 111, 113, 114, 128, 131,
133, 138, 142, 145, 161, 162,
167
loyal to de Gaulle 138
welcomes Alsatian refugees 49
Bastie
grounds-keeper in German
barracks at Arcachon, 1940 53
Bauer
Colonel, Commander in
Mont-de-Marsan 137
Berlin 26, 33, 86, 94, 159,
175-177
Bernadet
Commander J. M. 156
Bezos
Robert 5-8, 12, 13, 47, 64
Biarritz 124, 125
Bias 125
Billotte
General 151

Biscarosse, 125
Bloch
Marc 14
Bordeaux 5-7, 9, 12, 17, 24-28,
32, 44, 53, 54, 61, 62, 66, 70,
72, 78, 85, 95, 101, 107, 110,
113, 117, 123, 125, 126, 133,
139, 141, 143-145, 152, 160,
163, 173
Gestapo Headquarters in 74
Grand Rabbi of 143
Oppenheimer imprisoned in
66
Sephardic community of 27
Bostens 40
Boucau 125
Brachfeld 84-85
Bremen 38
Bretagne-de-Marsan 44, 52
Breton
Charles 16
Madame Veuve 16
Britain 12, 14, 28, 48, 54, 68,
69, 97
Brittany 12, 150
sub pens photographed in 60
Brousse
mayor of Grenade 133
Buchenwald 152
Bucy-le-Long 16
Buderich
U.S. camp at 148
Buglose 125, 147, 152, 155-157,
163
Bush
Vannevar 12
Cambrai 61
Canada 12, 38
and wheat production 165
convoys from 54
convoys from bombed from
Mont-de-Marsan 68
helps Poles emigrate 177
opposition to Franco 47
Cannes 61
Capbreton 125
Captieux 66
Casablanca 177
Casenave
Raymond, nom de guerre of
Laporterie 105, 113, 114
Cassutto
family 26
Rivka 169
Castel
family 169
Léo 16, 22, 26, 29

Casterat 180
Charente 152
Chebassier
Grenadois suspected by Weill
139
Cher
river 63
China 69
Churchill
Winston 9, 52, 60, 69, 123,
125
Classun 41, 111
Colinet 87
official at Pau 106, 107
Conqueré
Raphael 157
Crete 36
Curie
Frédéric Joliot 12
Czechoslovakia 27, 174
D'Obrenan
Franz Van Den Brouck 69
Dachau
boys from Grenade deported
to 134
Danneker
Theodor 85, 86
Darriet
Renée 15, 77, 97, 109, 112,
113
Renée warns Oppenheimer
about telephones 65
Daubas
Valentin and family 180
Daugnague 125, 163
Dax 21
De Champvallier
Lt. Col. 151
de Gaulle
Charles 5, 9, 11, 14, 47, 48,
50, 52, 60, 70, 106, 117, 127,
136, 138, 139, 144, 150, 155,
170
Charles, niece of 110
De Neuchèze
Captain 53
De Neufville
Hélène Rott 105
De Paul
St-Vincent 20
Deichmann
Hans, German resister 168
Delaunay
Gabriel 141
des Landes
Léon 113

Dessauer
  family 180
Dior
  Christian 166
Djibouti 43
Doenitz
  Karl 98
Dohse
  Friedrich 74, 100, 109, 112, 113
Dordogne 114
Drancy 86
Dubos
  Georges 42, 73, 79, 167
Duhort-Bachen 41
Dumartin
  Jean 19, 65, 109, 113
  visited by Gestapo 75
Dumoulin
  Georgette 77
Dupeyron 117, 119
  friend of Laporterie 78
Duportet
  Barthélémy 52-55
Duportets
  Henri 50
Dussarat
  Léonce 113
Duvignau
  Roger 162, 167
Eichmann
  Adolf 86, 87, 98
Eisenhower
  General Dwight D. 151-152
Elias
  family 108, 162
England 9, 25, 68, 69, 74, 97, 111, 118, 119, 120, 165
  opposition to Franco 46
Estang 135
Eugénie-les-Bains 41
Europe 9-11, 16, 25, 28, 46, 93, 94, 109, 124, 163
  threatened by communism, according to Laporterie 47
Falaise-Argentan pocket
  entrapment of Germans at 136
Farbos
  Joseph 74, 99
Fargue 40, 111
Fisher
  Fritz 110
Foerster
  Fritz 154
France 5, 7-12, 14-17, 19-21, 25-28, 32, 33, 37, 40-44, 47, 48, 52, 56, 59, 60, 70, 72, 79, 86, 90, 93, 94, 101, 103, 104, 108, 111, 112, 115, 117, 120, 127, 128, 136, 141, 142, 145, 147, 149, 150, 157, 158, 164, 165, 169, 173, 176, 177
  abandons ideals in 1940 170
  Anatole 7
  and beautiful villages 167

and International Red Cross 150
  British officers infiltrate 95
  ignorance in pains Laporterie 42
  invaded by French army 136
  Jews rounded up in 175
  Oppenheimer and Laporterie write reports on 65
  opposition to Franco 46
  remains although universe changes 46
  southwest region to be invaded 123
  unknown, honorable 167
  weakened by socialism, according to Laporterie 47
Franco
  Francisco 46
Frankfurt 151
Fredon
  Special Police Commissioner in Bordeaux, 1940 27
Galaber
  teacher protected by Laporterie 113
Gamberto
  fur merchant of Bordeaux 29, 33
Gandhi
  Mohandas 99
Gauthier
  Jean 101
Gave
  river 126
Geaune 90, 135
Geneva
  Convention of 160,
Germany 14, 15, 21, 26, 27, 30, 38, 53, 69, 72, 73, 87, 89, 93, 102, 103, 110, 112, 113, 114, 137, 147, 152, 162, 177
  (West) 165
  defeated 137
  supports Franco 46
Gers 16, 100
Goering
  Hermann 68
Goertz
  Hans 147, 150, 152-158, 162, 163, 165
Goethe
  Johann Wolfgang von 126
Gollancz
  Victor 159
Gourdon
  Germaine 33
Gourdon
  baker in Bascons 108
Grandclément
  Resistance chief in Bordeaux 113
Greece 29
Grenade 5, 6, 7, 16, 18, 23, 33, 35, 36, 40, 43, 44, 45, 52, 58,

61, 66, 70, 78, 81, 82, 83, 91-94, 96, 101, 103, 107, 111-113, 127, 129, 130, 133, 134, 137, 138, 139, 141, 144, 154, 160, 166, 168
Grenier
  false name of Yaeches 77, 101, 142
Grimand
  of Pau, protected by Laporterie 142
Guilhem
  Laure 40
  Madame Olympe 56, 87, 88, 89-91
Gurs 47, 108, 173, 174, 179
  Hannah Arendt imprisoned at 105
Hagetmau 44
Halifax 74
  Germans plan to bomb naval base at 68
Haute-Garonne 107
Hellman
  Peter 168
Henkel
  Major 176
Herz
  Alsatian who helped resistance 77, 80
Heyl
  Adam 147, 157, 162, 165
  Charles M. 176
Himmler
  Heinrich 86, 98
Hirschler
  René, Grand Rabbi of Strasbourg 179
Hitler
  Adolf 5, 8, 9-11, 13, 14, 19, 22, 26, 29, 33, 48, 50, 53, 54, 60, 68, 73, 79, 86, 88, 91, 93, 97, 99, 115, 117, 123, 132, 154, 160, 162, 163, 164
  Adolf, abandoned by Germans 137
  Adolf, Mercedes of bought by Vinet 161
  and Mein Kampf 68
  decides on the "Final Solution" for Jews 86
  early plans to harass Jews 25
  scheme to gain lebensraum in east 69
Ho Chi-Minh 171
Holland 39, 40
Hortense
  Madame, assistant store manager 80
Hortman
  German Police Commissioner in Bordeaux, 1940 27
Hossegor 125
India 101
Indo-China 56, 145, 161, 171

Israel 169
Italy 14, 99, 117
  supports Franco 46
Japan 14, 69
Jerusalem 169, 172
Julien
  Captain Third Algerian Rifles 151
Karp
  Israel 25-28
Khom
  family, Jewish refugees 135
Kielwasser
  René 49
Klarsfeld
  Serge 175
Koestler
  Arthur 174
Labouheyre 125, 155-158, 163
Lacoste
  Camille 67
Lafayssee
  Jeanne 16, 21, 30
Laffont
  Jean, false name of Yaeche 31
Lafontan
  Madame, hotel owner 135
Lamothe
  family 105-109
  family, escape from Bascons 109
Lamy
  Marie Claire, false name of Mme Malraux 69
Landes 6, 12, 16, 17, 21, 41, 43-45, 66, 79, 92, 108, 114, 123, 139, 146, 157, 158, 161, 167
Laos 171
Laporterie
  family 88
  Irène 85, 87, 88, 90, 132, 134, 162
  Laure 5, 131, 133, 160, 162
  Laure recovers her joie de vivre 167
  Nicole 162, 166
Larrieu
  Jean 59, 77, 81
  Mayor of Mont-de-Marsan 137
Larrivière 129, 130
Laroquette
  lawyer of Mont-de-Marsan 91, 92
Lauben
  Colonel Philip S. 150
Laval
  Pierre 14, 79, 86
Le Chambon-sur-Lignon 33, 94, 99, 144, 167, 177, 178
Le Houga 135
Le Mans 152
Le Penan 57, 59

estate near Grenade 51, 58, 118
Le Puy 177
Le Vernet 175
League of Nations 9
Lemée
  Madame Pierre 130
  Pierre 51, 58, 60, 118, 162
Leningrad 149
Léon 125
Lesage
  Gilbert 171, 172, 175
Lestelle-Betharram 76, 100, 108, 120, 142, 143
Levy
  Esther 169
Lille 61, 112
Limoges 30, 76
Lit 125
London 14
Lorraine 15, 19
Lot-et-Garonne 75
Louis XIV 78
Ludendorff
  Erich 38
Luttenbacher
  curé of Bartenheim 49
Lyon 33, 61, 87, 107, 137, 138, 177
Madrid 46
Malraux
  André 69, 70
  Clara 69
Marne 8
Marseille 61, 76, 77, 84, 151
Mauléon 101
Maura
  adjutant at Buglose 153
Meispleigt
  baker in Bascons 108
Mellows
  Captain T. A. leads attack on Germans 137
Meneteau
  Madame, concierge in German barracks at Arcachon, 1940 53, 55
Merignac
  airport 9
Meyer
  Chief Delegate of ICRC 164
Milles 175
Mimizan-Plage 125
Model
  Field Marshal Walther 148
Monnet
  colonel in Resistance at Pau 122, 123
Mont-de-Marsan 6, 7, 8, 13, 15, 18, 19, 22, 30, 35-37, 39, 42, 43, 45, 47, 48, 51, 54-62, 64-68, 71, 73, 74, 77, 78, 81, 83, 90, 91, 93, 95, 98, 101, 110, 111, 113, 118, 120, 123, 127, 130, 131, 133, 134,

136-138, 144, 146, 147, 156, 157, 163, 167
  and Portuguese corrida 64
  Germans build new runways for airport at 68
  Laporterie escapes from 81
  Laporterie founds first branch in 44
  Poidlouë takes refuge in 58
Montgaillard 41
Montgomery
  British general who terrorized Aquitaine 134
Montreal 74
Moulin
  Jean 144
Mourgues
  Pierre 27
Muret 106
Mussolini
  Benito 98
Myredé
  Chateau de, near Grenade 57, 59, 112, 131
Napoléon
  Bonaparte 95, 121
Napoléon III 78
Netter
  Rabbi 63
New York 169
Noë 175
Normandy 127, 137
North Africa 9, 75, 91, 93, 97, 124
North America 30
Notre-Dame-de-Rugby 111
Nuremberg 159
  trials 86
Olivier
  Colonel 51
Oppenheimer
  Abel 9, 64, 65, 70, 79, 95, 163
  Abel and Blanche, papers not marked Jewish 66
  Abel works for Germans 67
  arrested 66
  Blanche 66
Oradour-sur-Glane 99, 129
Papon
  Maurice 109
Paris 5-8, 11, 20, 22, 24, 28, 36, 47, 57, 61, 64, 69, 70, 74, 79, 86, 87, 107, 112, 119, 138, 151, 166-171, 175, 176
Pau 8, 37, 47, 55, 61, 76, 83, 87, 88, 90, 91, 92-95, 105, 107, 108, 114, 119-121, 124, 125, 127, 166, 173
Paulus
  Friedrich 97
Pêcheur
  Jules 73
Perlberger
  Max 84

Pétain
  Henri Philippe 5, 7-10, 12, 14, 15, 18, 21, 26, 37, 50, 52, 63, 79, 88, 90, 93, 128, 170
Piaf
  Edith 69
Pills
  Jacques 69
Piot
  Jean, executed for illegal crossing 75
Pissos 125
Poidloue
  Charles 57-60, 69, 74, 111
  Julienne 57-59, 112
Pointis Mme 77
Poland 26, 27, 48, 87, 96, 97, 174
Pont-de-Bats 137
Pope Pius XII 154
Portugal 27, 176
Pouzelgues
  Jean 52-54, 161
Pradervand
  Jean Pierre 150-152
Proëres
  family 139
  Madame Veuve 88
  Marie-Louise 133
Proust
  Marcel 69
Puy-de-Dôme 100
Pyrénées 17, 41, 101, 106, 180
Quilbeuf
  assistant to Laporterie 163
Ravensbruck
  women's camp at 110
Remagen
  U.S. camp at 148
Rémy
  Colonel 62, 161
Rennes 150
Renung 41, 117
Rheinberg
  U.S. camp at 148, 149
Rioux
  Jean Pierre 171
Rivalin
  Jean, describes Toulouse during war 95
Riveil
  Colonel 87
Rivesaltes 175
Rommel
  Erwin 97, 99
Roosevelt
  Franklin 11, 12
Rothschild
  family 70, 78
Ruhr 117
Russia 9, 14, 28, 69, 97, 99, 101, 108, 117, 177
  opposes Franco 47
Sabres 125
Safaty

family 30, 76
Saint John 74
Sartre
  Jean-Paul 14
  on France 47
Sauckel
  Fritz 159, 160
Schiller
  Johann Christoph Friedrich von 126
Schmahling
  Julius 178
Schoff
  Lieutenant Walter 130
Schwanitz
  George 154
Seignosse 125
Sicily 108
Smith
  General W. Bedell 151
Solzhenitsyn
  Alexander 99
Soubeiray
  Lieutenant, Third Algerian Rifles 151
Soustons 125
Spain 27, 37, 47, 60, 61, 87, 101, 123, 137, 173
  Jews transit en route to North America 176
St-Cyprien 175
St-Etienne 94
St-Germain
  Chanoine Jean-Baptiste 154
St-Laurent
  Yves 166
St-Maurice 41
St-Nazaire 52, 60
St Paul 117
St-Paul-les-Dax 152
St-Sever 58, 81
St-Vincent-de-Paul 21, 154
Stalin
  Josef 60, 125
Stalingrad 91, 97
Stockelings
  Werner 165
Stoppler
  M., Jewish refugee 135
Stumpfegger
  Ludwig 110
Switzerland 60
Sydney 74
Tachon
  and German spies in Aire 104
  André 22-25, 54, 55, 60, 62, 67, 70, 75, 77, 78-81, 83, 100-101, 102-104, 138, 140
Tarbes 77, 114, 115
Thompson
  Dorothy 159
Thorée-les-Pins 152, 155
Tomasini
  assistant prefect at Pau 122
Toulouse 66, 87, 95, 96, 98,

105, 107, 114, 127, 129, 138, 157, 176
  resistance in 95
Troomé
  André 98, 99, 178, 179
Tulle, 136
United States 11, 14, 25, 38, 46, 69, 75
  and wheat production 165
Verdun 7, 8
  Raoul Laporterie and father meet at, 38
Vichy 10, 11, 15, 18, 20, 21, 26, 29, 32, 33, 50, 52, 54, 62, 65, 70, 83, 86-88, 91-94, 100, 102, 103, 108, 112, 136, 142, 170, 174-180
  moles in government 52
  permits Jews to leave in 1942 177
Vielle
  René 58, 107, 128-131, 133
Viet Nam 56, 161, 171
Villeneuve 81
Vinet
  Henri 67, 87, 94, 95, 100, 101, 102-104, 115, 116, 119, 120, 124, 126, 161
von Blaskowitz 129, 135, 137
  German commander in southwest 129
Von Falkenhayn
  Erich 37, 38
Wannsee 175, 177
  conference at 86
Wanzek
  John 154
Weill
  Colonel Albert 87, 95, 96, 139
  seeks vengeance 138, 139
Weygand
  Maxime 11
Wilhelm II
  Kaiser of Germany 40
Wittenberg
  Charles 96
Yad Vashem 167, 168, 172
Yaeche
  family 26-33, 35, 63, 72, 73, 75-78, 85, 86, 110, 120, 142, 145, 160, 162, 163
Zavidowics
  merchant helped by Laporterie 87, 88, 90, 91, 92
Zeldin
  Theodor 166

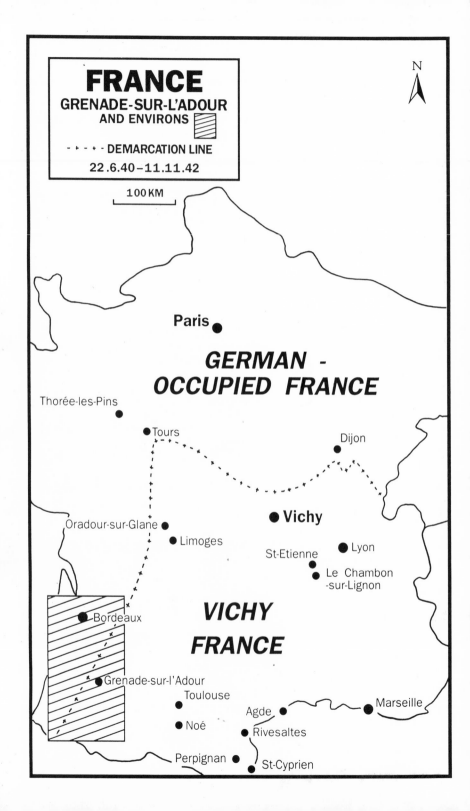